Lakes, Ponds, and Temporary Pools

DAVID JOSEPHS

EXPLORING ECOSYSTEMS

FRANKLIN WATTS
A Division of Grolier Publishing
New York   London   Hong Kong   Sydney
Danbury, Connecticut

Note to Readers: Terms defined in glossary are **bold** in the text. In most cases, measurements are given in both metric and English units. Wherever measurements are given in only one system, the units provided are the most appropriate for that situation.

Photographs ©: Bob Clemenz Photography: 13 (Bob & Suzanne Clemenz); Landslides Aerial Photography: 15 (Alex S. McLean); Photo Researchers: 45 (Tom Branch), 103 (B. Derig), 27, 63 (Jack Dermid), 29 (Michael P. Gadomski), 95 (Valerie Giles), 97 (Jeff Lepore), 23 top (Maslowski), 23 bottom (Tom McHugh), 73 (William H. Mullins), 75 (Hugh Spencer/ National Audubon Society), 34 (M. I. Walker/Science Source), 77 (Jeanne White/National Audubon Society), 25 (D. P. Wilson/Science Source); Superstock, Inc.: 92; Tom Vezo: 57, 59, 65; Tony Stone Images: cover (Cosmo Condina), 61 (Darrell Gulin), 56 (Kim Heacox), 48 (Kevin Summers); Visuals Unlimited: 50 (Bill Beatty), 43 (Patrice Ceisel).

Illustrations by Bob Italiano, and Steve Savage
Book interior design and pagination by Carole Desnoes

Visit Franklin Watts on the Internet at:
http://publishing.grolier.com

Library of Congress Cataloging-in-Publication Data

Josephs, David
    Lakes, ponds, and temporary pools / David Josephs
        p. cm. — (Exploring ecosystems)
    Includes bibliographical references and index.
    Summary: Explains the importance of preserving and protecting slow-moving water habitats and provides instructions for related projects and activities.
        ISBN 0-531-11698-0 (lib. bdg.)   0-531-16506-X (pbk.)
    1. Freshwater ecology—Studying and teaching—Activity programs— Juvenile literature [1. Freshwater ecology. 2. Ecology.] I. Title. II. Series.
QH541.5.F7R68   2000
577.63'078—dc21   99-057578

Contents

Introduction

MOST OF US HAVE PROBABLY VISITED A lake or pond to swim, fish, boat, or just relax. Lakes and ponds are also good places to take in the sights and sounds of the natural world. However, these bodies of quiet water are more than just fun places to visit. They are home to a variety of plant and animal life. Although some of these creatures are familiar to us, many others are not.

When you begin to explore the life in lakes, ponds, and temporary pools, you are embarking on an adventure into the ways plant and animal life has adapted to a world of quiet waters. As you read this book and do the activities, you'll begin to understand how all the components of an **ecosystem**—the organisms and the environment they live in—are connected.

Lakes and ponds present unique challenges to the plants and animals that live here. For example, plants that grow in the water must adapt to lower light levels because the sunlight they need for **photosynthesis**—the process by which plants turn sunlight into energy—is filtered out by the water. Just like the animals on land, animals that live in the water must be able to get oxygen. The animals that live in quiet waters have solved this problem in a number of ways. Some have gills or special breathing tubes, while others absorb oxygen through their skin.

Lakes and ponds are **lentic,** or standing-water, ecosystems. Lakes and large ponds have three zones. The shallow-water area along the shore is the **littoral zone. Emergent plants,** which have their roots in the water but their stems and leaves in the air, grow in this area. The **limnetic zone** is the open-water area away from the shore. This area extends as far as sunlight penetrates, and it is where the larger fish spend most of their time. The **profundal zone** is the deepest zone of a lake. It begins where the limnetic zone ends. No light reaches this zone, so there are no plants here. Some ponds and shallow lakes do not have a profundal zone.

Time for a Change

The location of a lake, pond, or temporary pool is the result of geological activity, human activity, or a combination of the two. Many lakes and ponds have been around for thousands of years. Most of them were formed by glacial action, or other geological events. Other lakes and ponds have come about much more recently. Lakes and ponds are dynamic environments that are constantly changing.

Regardless of how they were created, all lakes and ponds undergo succession—a process of change from one type of ecosystem to another. Some lakes and ponds undergo this change very quickly. For example, an earthquake might create a tilt in the landscape that causes a lake to drain very quickly. However, for most lakes and ponds, succession is gradual—it can take hundreds, thousands, or even millions of years. As these bodies of water fill with sediments brought in by streams or rainfall, the conditions in them begin to change. The water becomes shallower and, over time, different species of plants and animals move in. Given enough time, the lake or pond will cease to exist. Figuring out where in this aging process a lake or pond is can help scientists understand it better.

The activities of humans also have an effect on lakes and ponds. It's easy to see how houses near the water's edge might affect the water. But human activities far from the shoreline can also influence aquatic creatures. Activities in a **watershed**—the land that drains into a lake or pond—might bring pollutants, such as toxic chemicals, pesticides, excessive silt, warm water, and debris, into the water. Any of these pollutants has the potential to change the conditions of a lake or pond and may affect the creatures that live there.

Looking for Connections: It's Ecological

Ecosystems are complex, so finding the connections between the plants and animals that live there and their surroundings can be a great challenge. This book has a variety of investigations and projects designed to help you explore the **ecology**—the study of interrelationships between organisms and their environment—of lakes, ponds, and temporary pools. The activities cover a range of subjects including biology, chemistry, physics, mathematics, and geography. Some are simple, others are more complex. Some activities are designed for individuals, while others are best carried out with friends or fellow students. Some of the activities will require extended periods of time and observation.

The aim of this book is to stimulate your curiosity and guide your observations of lakes and ponds. Science, particularly ecology, is based on asking provocative questions of nature and finding ways to get nature to provide the answers. To do this, you need to go outside and get dirty!

As you become familiar with the nature of your local lakes and ponds, you will also become aware of the many ways in which human activities have a negative impact on the health of some lakes and ponds. Perhaps you will be able to use your knowledge to improve the quality of these lakes and ponds. You may even decide to help establish a local lake or pond association so that others can work with you to make the waters healthier.

Playing It Safe

Lakes, ponds, and temporary pools are fun places to explore and investigate, but they can also be hazardous. Even in summer, deep lakes can be cold enough to cause **hypothermia.** In winter, ice coverings can vary in thickness, making it easy to fall through. Follow these rules to protect yourself and others:

- Always wear a personal flotation device when you are out in a boat or canoe.
- Always let someone know where you will be and when you expect to return.
- Always snorkel or scuba dive with a partner. Also, use a dive flag to warn boaters that you are in the area.
- The intensity of the sun can be increased when sunlight is reflected off the water. Wear waterproof sunscreen and keep track of your sun exposure.
- Wear sandals or old sneakers when wading to protect your feet. There may be broken bottles or sharp rocks on the lake bottom.
- If you will be out in a motorboat, learn the rules for safe boating.

If you follow these rules you should have a great time (and a rewarding one) as you make your way through the projects and investigations that follow.

Make a Note of It!

For many of the projects in this book, you'll need to keep track of a lot of important information. So do what scientists do—write it down in a journal. Reading over your notes may help you see connections that you missed when you were out in the field. Here are some of the things you'll definitely want to record:

- date, time, location
- surrounding area (land-use patterns, soil type, erosion)
- weather conditions (Is it sunny, rainy, or sort of in-between? Try to estimate the percentage of cloud cover. What is the air temperature and the water temperature? When was the last time it rained?)

Here are some other things to look for:

- What creatures do you see and what behaviors are they engaging in?
- Check the site at various times of the day (and even at night using a flashlight). Do you notice any differences?
- Do you observe any mating habits? Under what conditions?
- How long does it take for eggs to hatch? Does it take longer in the shade than in the sunlight? Once hatched, how long does it take the young to reach maturity?

Photographs and drawings are also a great way to keep track of what you find. It's a good idea to include these in your journal too. You may also want to enter some of the information you collect into data sheets or tables. They'll help you keep your data organized. You'll find samples of these throughout this book.

Looking back on your records, can you detect patterns that link certain animal activities and behaviors with environmental conditions?

CHAPTER 1

Quiet Waters: Lakes and Ponds

LAKES AND PONDS ARE OFTEN STRUNG like beads on a string of rivers and streams. But unlike rivers and streams, lakes and ponds are bodies of quiet water with relatively little current moving through them. The major movements in these waters are waves caused by the winds that blow over them.

There are many different types of lakes and ponds, and most are home to many living things. The plants, animals, and microorganisms living in a lake or pond interact with each other and with their surroundings. The study of these interactions is called ecology. Exploring these interconnections is the work of **ecologists** and the challenge of this book.

We generally think of lakes as large, deep bodies of water and ponds as smaller, shallower bodies. This is usually the case, but to a **limnologist,** a scientist who studies freshwater environments, the definitions are much more complex.

Limnologists classify some waters commonly called lakes as large ponds because they are shallow. Other waters may have a small surface area but be quite deep. Most people would call them ponds, but limnologists think of them as lakes.

The classifications of quiet, standing waters used by limnologists are based on physical, chemical, and biological characteristics.

How Did It Get Here?

In the past, as glaciers inched across the landscape, they carved out basins in which ponds and lakes later formed. Most lakes in the world were formed as the result of glacial action. Other geological forces also create basins that can hold water. **Tectonic** forces cause changes in Earth's crust, and have created some of the oldest and deepest lakes in the world.

Not all lakes and ponds arose during ancient times. Volcanic forces, which have helped create some of the clearest lakes in the world, continue to be an important force in creating lakes and ponds. Sometimes, as flowing rivers change course, a bend in the river may be cut off by a change in flow, leaving behind an **oxbow lake** (see Figure 1 on the next page).

Earthquakes and landslides may also cause rock and other debris to build up and create a dam across a river. If the flow of water is cut off, a lake will form behind the dam. In some areas, the ground is made of limestone, a type of rock that dissolves easily in water. When water enters—through rainfall or from a river—the limestone deposits dissolve. Basins that trap water may form and, eventually, become lakes or ponds.

The Great Lakes—Superior, Michigan, Huron, Erie, and Ontario—are examples of the many North American lakes with beds carved out by glaciers. Lake Tahoe, on the

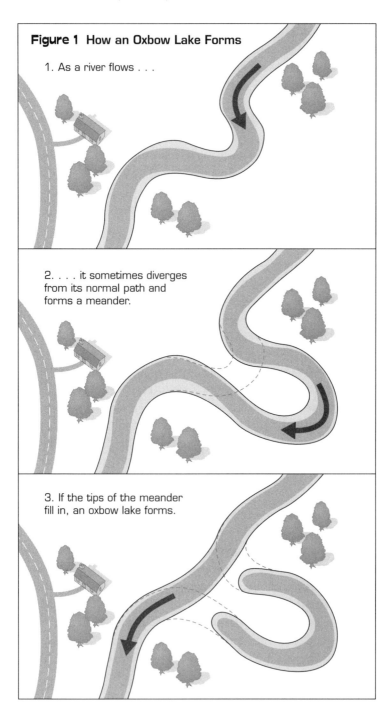

Figure 1 How an Oxbow Lake Forms

1. As a river flows . . .

2. . . . . it sometimes diverges from its normal path and forms a meander.

3. If the tips of the meander fill in, an oxbow lake forms.

border of California and Nevada, formed in a valley that was created along a geological fault line. Fault lines are deep cracks in the Earth's crust. Lava flows dammed streams that flowed through the fault, creating the lake.

The Finger Lakes in New York State originated as riverbeds that were dammed by the debris, or **glacial moraine deposits,** of receding glaciers. Crater Lake in Oregon had a more exotic beginning: Water filled the hollowed-out bowl, or **caldera,** at the center of an extinct volcano. Lake Malheur and Lake Harney in Oregon also have volcanic origins. In their case, lava flows formed dams across rivers. Reelfoot Lake in western Tennessee was formed after the New Madrid earthquake of 1811–1812 caused blocks of earth to shift and form a basin that then filled with water.

Crater Lake in Oregon was formed by a volcanic eruption.

Human-made lakes are created when people build dams on rivers and streams. Dams are built for a variety of reasons: for flood control, to generate electrical power, to provide a water supply, or to create a recreational area. Life in these reservoirs may be abundant, but it is seldom as diverse and rich as that found in natural lakes and ponds. If you have a chance to visit Chattanooga, Tennessee, be sure to see the great Chattanooga Aquarium. It focuses on the Tennessee River and the many lakes that formed behind the dams the Tennessee Valley Authority (TVA) built along the river. The Aquarium also has also devoted a great deal of space to a discussion of rivers and lakes of the world. The exhibits highlight fish and other aquatic creatures that are found in these waterways.

A lake or pond can develop whenever natural or human-made forces create a basin that can hold water. Water is always evaporating from the surface of quiet water. If at least as much water enters a basin as is lost, the lake persists. But if more water is lost than enters, the lake shrinks. In desert areas where there are very large but shallow basins, lakes may form in the spring after snowmelt or heavy rains and later evaporate. These temporary lakes are called **playa lakes.**

Lakes and Ponds in North America

Whether they are deep or shallow, most lakes and ponds in the northeastern and north-central parts of the United States and Canada are glacial in origin. Minnesota has more than 40,000 natural lakes larger than 4 hectares (10 acres); Michigan has about 11,000; and Wisconsin has around 8,700.

Lakes and ponds in the southeastern United States are generally shallow. They were created by receding oceans, meandering rivers that created oxbow lakes, earthquakes that caused depressions, or limestone that dissolved away and left a sinkhole that filled with water. There are some 955,000 natural lakes in the southeast-

Minnesota is home to many glacial lakes.

ern United States. Seventy-eight percent of them are in Florida, and about 12 percent are in Louisiana.

Natural lakes in the Southwest are rare and are often the remains of ancient sea beds. They tend to be shallow and rich in minerals. Their water comes from runoff that drains broad areas of land into these shallow basins. A rise in groundwater level and the development of springs may also bring water into these basins.

During the geologic time period called the Pliocene, about 1 to 10 million years ago, numerous large lakes were scattered throughout the Mojave and Great Basin areas of the United States. In northwestern Utah, Lake Bonneville once covered about 52,000 square kilometers (20,000 square miles) and had a shoreline of more than 4,020 kilometers (2,500 miles) at high water, and a maximum depth of nearly 304 meters (1,000 feet). The Great Salt Lake in Utah is a remnant of Lake Bonneville. It covers roughly 5,000 square kilometers (1,930 sq. mi.) and

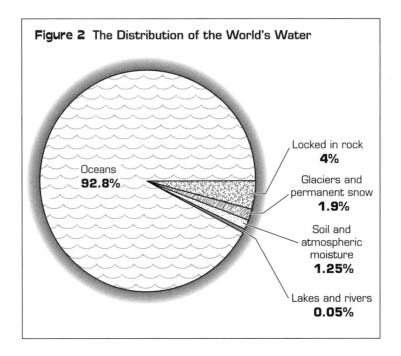

Figure 2 The Distribution of the World's Water

Oceans
92.8%

Locked in rock
4%

Glaciers and permanent snow
1.9%

Soil and atmospheric moisture
1.25%

Lakes and rivers
0.05%

has a depth of only 9 meters (30 ft.). Some limnologists might say it should really be called Great Salt Pond!

The lakes of North America, including the Great Lakes and the Canadian lakes—Lake Winnipeg, Lake Athabaska, Great Bear Lake, and Great Slave Lake—hold about 25 percent of all the freshwater in the world. The volume of water in lakes is about ten times the amount of water in the atmosphere. The volume of water in lakes is about 100 times that of the water in rivers and streams at any given moment (see Figure 2).

Through evaporation and precipitation, water falls onto the land as rainfall or snow and returns to the ocean via the vast network of streams and rivers. On the way, some of the water finds a temporary home in lakes and ponds. Although some of the water that enters lakes and ponds evaporates into the atmosphere, a great deal of it leaves through an outlet and eventually reaches the ocean (see Figure 3).

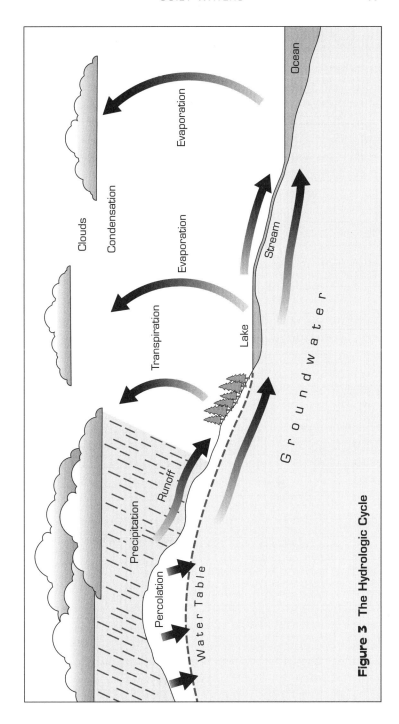

Figure 3 The Hydrologic Cycle

Generally, rainwater and snowmelt hold relatively few dissolved materials. But as rain and snowmelt flow over land, they dissolve minerals and carry them into lakes and ponds. Water bubbling up from groundwater as springs may also contain dissolved materials. Over time, the lakes and ponds become rich with these materials. Incoming water from rich soils also brings **nutrients.** The water flowing into a lake or pond may also bring mineral salts.

In some areas, such as the southwestern United States, heavy evaporation concentrates the minerals so the lakes there may contain higher-than-average levels of mineral salts. Such **alkaline** water is unfit to drink, as is the case with the Great Salt Lake.

The chemistry of lake water is often greatly affected by the dissolved minerals, nutrients, and other chemicals that are carried into the water. The underlying geological features of the lake site are also partially responsible for the water's characteristics. Because water chemistry and geology vary so widely, there are many different kinds of lakes. As a result, limnologists have developed a fairly complex system for classifying these bodies of water. Because different kinds of plants and animals prefer, or tolerate, different chemical conditions, certain species are generally associated with each lake type. As you will learn, the diversity of life in a lake also influences the way limnologists classify it.

Lakes Around the World

Large lakes, of course, are not limited to North America. Lake Baikal in Russia is the deepest freshwater lake in the world. The Great Rift Valley of East Africa is home to a string of distinctive lakes—some of them are freshwater and others are quite **brackish,** meaning they are mixed with saltwater. Some brackish lakes, such as Lake Nakuru in Kenya, are home to huge flocks of flamingos. The freshwater lakes, such as Lake Tanganyika and Lake Nyasa in Tanzania, boast thriving fish populations. Lake Victoria on the border of Kenya and Uganda was formed by tectonic forces, as was Lake Titicaca, which lies high in the Andes Mountains of South America. There are also many large human-made lakes around the world. Kimberly Lake in South Africa is one of the deepest artificial lakes in the world. It formed in an abandoned diamond mine.

A Matter of Layers

Water is an unusual substance because it behaves in ways that are quite different from most other liquids. Water is a molecule made up of two hydrogen atoms and one oxygen atom. The way these atoms are arranged gives water its many unique properties, including its **density.** The density of a substance is a measure of the amount of matter found in a certain volume of the substance. It indicates how tightly the atoms in the substance are packed. Most liquids occupy a smaller space as they cool—in other words, they become denser. But water has its greatest density at 4° Celsius (39.2° Fahrenheit). Below that temperature, its density decreases. Ice at 0°C (32°F) is less dense than water at 0°C (32°F). That is why ice floats on water. This relationship between water and ice influences the seasonal changes that occur within a lake (see Figure 4 on the next page).

As spring winds blow across the lake's surface, water accumulates on the downwind side. This colder water sinks and passes across the bottom of the lake, causing circulation of the water in the lake. For a while, the whole lake is fairly uniform in density.

As the spring winds decline, the sun warms the water. The warmer, lighter surface water floats above the colder, denser, deeper waters. Summer winds generally aren't strong enough to cause the two layers to mix. Over the course of the summer, the top layer of water—the **epilimnion**—gradually grows warmer, while the bottom

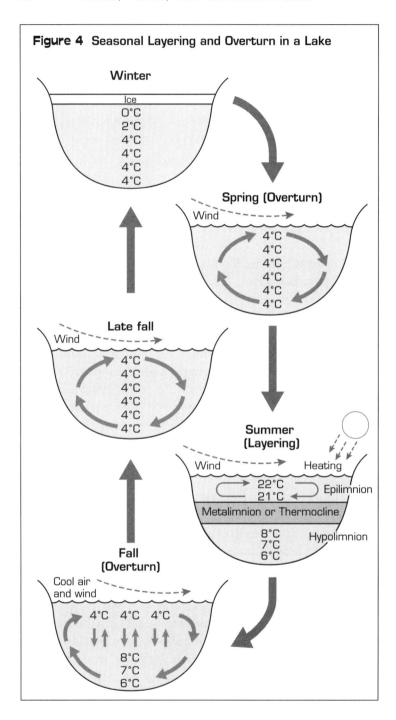

Figure 4 Seasonal Layering and Overturn in a Lake

layer—the **hypolimnion**—remains cold. At the point where the two layers of different densities meet, a transition layer called the **metalimnion** forms. Here the upper and lower layers exchange heat.

In large lakes, the metalimnion, also called the **thermocline,** is usually thinner than the epilimnion. In smaller ponds, the epilimnion may extend all the way to the bottom, completely eliminating the hypolimnion. The layering of water according to temperature and density is a very important feature of lakes and ponds. It sets limits for the different forms of life that live in each body of water.

Bass or Trout:
Which Fish Lives Where?

Like humans, fish need oxygen to stay alive. They get this oxygen from the water itself, in the form of dissolved oxygen. Different types of fish require different amounts of oxygen. For example, trout do best in water that has a lot of oxygen, but bass do not require as much oxygen. It is the relative ability of the hypolimnion to hold dissolved oxygen in summer that largely determines whether a lake can support a particular kind of fish. Figure 5 on the next page shows some common lake fishes.

Because warm water holds less dissolved oxygen than cold water, trout do best in cold-water lakes, while bass tend to live in warm-water lakes. In fact, cold-water lakes with a lot of dissolved oxygen are sometimes called trout lakes, while warmer lakes are called bass lakes.

During the summer, trout often avoid a lake's surface waters. The surface is the warmest part of a lake and may not hold enough dissolved oxygen for these fish. Instead, trout spend most of their time down in the hypolimnion, which usually contains a fairly rich supply of oxygen. But this may not be the case if the lake contains large numbers of bacteria and invertebrates—animals without a backbone. These creatures need oxygen too. They may

Figure 5 Some Common Lake Fishes

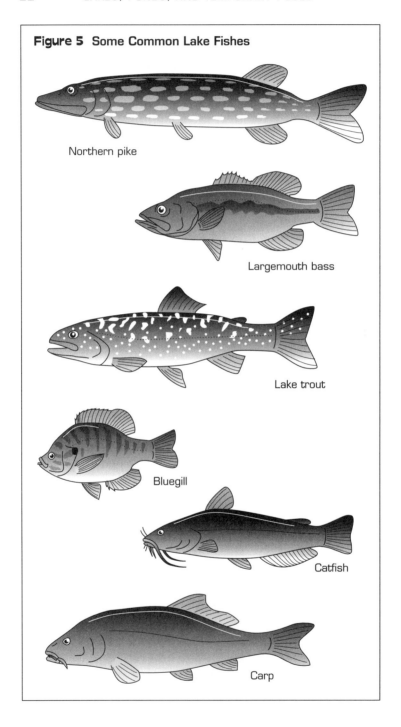

Northern pike

Largemouth bass

Lake trout

Bluegill

Catfish

Carp

Smallmouth bass live in warm waters with low oxygen levels.

Lake trout live in cold water that is rich in dissolved oxygen.

deplete the oxygen in the hypolimnion, making it difficult for trout to survive. Bass would do better in this
environment. In some lakes, bass can live in the epilimnion all summer long.

Cold-water lakes are often deep and large with rocky
bottoms. They are usually surrounded by thin, relatively
sterile soils. In the deepest areas of a lake, the cold water
contains abundant oxygen throughout the summer, but
the surface layer may be much warmer and have little
oxygen. Under such conditions, the fish can get the oxygen they need at the bottom of the lake. However, because
there are generally few nutrients entering the lake, it
can't support large populations of the living things fish
like to eat, such as insects or other invertebrates. As a result, these lakes have relatively small populations of
fishes—primarily trout. Hence their name—trout lakes.

In such lakes you will find many members of the
trout family including salmon, lake trout, chars, ciscoes,
and graylings. Trout lakes usually support less than 23
kilograms (50 pounds) of fish per surface hectare (2.5
acres). Aquatic plant species are also much more limited
in both number and diversity. Scientists call trout lakes
oligotrophic, from the Latin *oligo* meaning "little" and
trophic meaning "food."

Other groups of lakes are found in areas with more
fertile soils. They are of medium to shallow depth and
have variable surface areas. These lakes may form layers
in the summer, but even the deep water does not contain
enough oxygen to support trout. These lakes are rich in
plant and invertebrate life, and can support an abundant
fish population. The fish that live here can withstand
higher temperatures and need less oxygen than trout.
These fish are usually members of the bass family including largemouth bass, crappies, bluegills, and sunfish.
Other fish families that survive here include channel catfish, bullheads, carp, and suckers.

Scientists call these lakes **eutrophic.** The relatively
high availability of food allows a rich variety of plants

and animals to live in them. These lakes normally produce far more fish per surface area than oligotrophic lakes.

There are also lakes where available oxygen and food is somewhere between oligotrophic and eutrophic. These lakes are classified as **mesotrophic** from the Latin *meso* meaning "middle." Mesotrophic lakes have some growth of plants and **algae**—one-celled plant-like microorganisms. They also have some accumulation of silt, soil, and other sediments. Both cold-water and warm-water fish species may be present.

Through succession, lakes and ponds are always aging. As a part of that process, lakes move from being oligotrophic toward being mesotrophic and eutrophic. This change may take place over long periods of time, or it may be accelerated by either natural or human-made processes. For example, construction around a lake or

Microscopic algae and diatoms are commonly found in lakes and ponds.

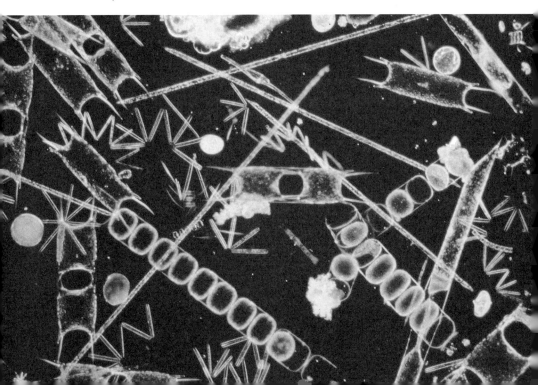

pond can cause an increase in erosion—the wearing away of Earth's surface. As sediments are carried into the water, the lake or pond may become shallower and the amount of nutrients in the water may increase, speeding up the natural aging process. As you explore the waters of your area, ask yourself where in this process your lake or pond fits.

Ponds: Cradles of Life

Ponds are generally smaller and shallower than lakes, but they share many of the same water-layering characteristics, and they are usually much richer in the dissolved nutrients that help support life. Although some living things can be found in almost all lakes and ponds, the greatest diversity of aquatic life tends to be concentrated in the warm, nutrient-rich waters of shallow ponds.

Shallow ponds with sandy or muddy bottoms support a variety of aquatic plants. Plants such as water milfoil and *Sagittaria* are rooted on the bottom and spread their leaves in midwater. Other plants such as water lily and water shield are also rooted on the bottom, but their leaves float on the water's surface. In very shallow water, emergent plants such as cattails and arrowheads grow up out of the water. Different plant parts provide food and shelter to a great variety of aquatic animals including ostracods, tiny water fleas called *Daphnia*, scuds, and snails. In turn, these animals provide food for small fishes, which are then eaten by larger fishes (see Figure 6 on page 28).

The warm waters and abundant nutrients in ponds can give rise to **blooms**—rapid overgrowths of green algae. Some algae is attached to rocks or other materials at the bottom of the pond or to plant stems and leaves, while some drifts in the water. A variety of microscopic animals feed on the algae and may multiply so rapidly that they seem to bloom too. Blooms may change the color and clarity of the water.

White water lilies typically have round leaves and white flowers.

Ponds are created by many of the same factors that create lakes. They may also form when beavers build dams across small streams. These ponds usually have silty or muddy bottoms, are relatively shallow, and support a large diversity of plant and animal life. Trees flooded by the rising water die and create nesting sites for birds, such as herons. Woodpeckers carve out holes that are later used by swallows and other birds. Many of these birds feed on the adult aquatic insects that began their life in the waters below.

In many parts of North America, farmers have created ponds to provide water for livestock, fire protection, and recreation. Many aquatic plants and animals find their way to such ponds by hitchhiking on the feet of

Figure 6 A Simple Food Web

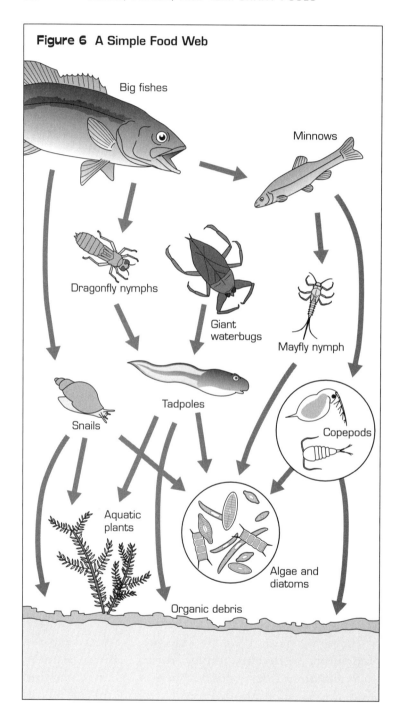

A typical human-made farm pond

ducks, herons, and other aquatic birds. Farmers themselves may introduce fishes, such as bluegills and catfish.
However, human-made ponds seldom achieve the diversity of life found in natural ponds.

Exploring and investigating the many habitats and
life forms in ponds can be exciting and fun. Later chap-
ters in this book will lead you through a variety of such
investigations to help you discover the adaptations that
plants and animals have made to living in freshwater.

It's a good idea to concentrate your studies on one
body of water. That way you'll really get to know it. Find
a lake or pond near your house so you can visit often.
But be sure to check out some other sites as well. Visiting
other lakes and ponds will help you get some perspective
on what makes your study site unique.

Temporary Pools: A Race to Maturity

Small, temporary ponds may appear in some places after heavy rains. In parts of North America, **vernal pools** form in spring after the snow melts. As air temperatures rise, the **evaporation** rate—the rate at which water leaves the pool and goes into the atmosphere—increases. At the same time, less water flows into the pool. As a result, the pond begins to shrink and may disappear completely by late summer or early fall. In some areas, temporary pools may appear briefly during the rainy season or after summer thunderstorms.

These temporary ponds or pools will not support fish, so they are the ideal places for small animals, such as young wood frogs, mole salamanders, and fairy shrimp, to grow up. They are not free of predators, however. Spotted or wood turtles feed on salamander eggs, while herons feast on tadpoles. Many aquatic insects—including water scorpions and dragonfly **larvae**—are also predatory. In other bodies of water, larvae must avoid a greater variety of predators.

The unique environment of a temporary pool poses another challenge—the animals must become adults before the water disappears. Some animals complete their life cycle in the diminishing water and develop a drought-resistant egg or spore that can survive until the water returns. Many mosquitoes fit this pattern. Their eggs may lie dormant for several years until water covers them and allows them to hatch.

The greatest challenges for survival, however, generally come from competition for food and oxygen as the pools shrink and an increasing number of individuals are crowded into less space. If the pool becomes too small too quickly, all the offspring in a particular year may be lost!

Temporary pools are unique and challenging aquatic habitats that are quickly disappearing as they are drained or filled to make space for homes and businesses.

Consequently, some states have passed laws to help identify and certify these pools and protect them from thoughtless development. Students have played a major role in identifying temporary pools and teaching others about these small ecological treasures. In fact, one group of high school students has developed a book and slide program about these pools. The program is called *Wicked Big Puddles*. In a later chapter you'll learn how you can study temporary pools in your area.

CHAPTER 2

Creatures of Habitat: Animal Life in Lakes and Ponds

Lakes and ponds are home to a wide variety of animals. Each group of animals has developed adaptations that make it possible for them to live in aquatic environments. For instance, fish have fins to help them navigate through the water and gills to help them take in oxygen. Many of the birds that live along the shores of lake sand ponds have long legs for wading and long, slender beaks for poking around in the mud for food. To avoid predators, some insects take in oxygen through a breathing tube. They can poke it up above the water's surface while they remain safely underwater. You can discover some of these animal adaptations by observing the creatures that live in the quiet waters near your home.

Observing with Face Mask and Snorkel

An easy way to observe the creatures in a lake or pond is by slowly swimming around with a face mask and snorkel. Swim fins will help you move faster and more easily, but they are not essential. It is important that you choose a properly fitting face mask, however. When shopping for a mask, hold the mask tightly to your face, inhale, hold your breath, and let go of the mask. The mask should remain firmly in place. If it does not, water will leak in while you are snorkeling.

Snorkels come in a variety of models. The best snorkels have a curved, soft-rubber mouthpiece that fits in your mouth and a straight tube that extends above the water's surface. Air in the tube keeps water from entering your mouth when you dive. If you do get water in the tube, a quick burst of breath should blast it out.

Adjust the tube so that it is in the air when you swim horizontally in the water. Most snorkels have a rubber tube holder that fits on the strap of a face mask and holds the snorkel in place. If you take some time to learn how to use your snorkeling equipment, you will have countless hours of exciting underwater observing.

If you sunburn easily, be sure to wear a T-shirt and waterproof sunblock or waterproof sun-screen lotion. You can even wear pajama bottoms in the water to help protect yourself from the sun.

Carry some white stones, or stones wrapped in aluminum foil, and drop them on the bottom to create a trail. You can follow your trail over and over and keep track of the creatures—and their homes—that you see along the way. Keep mental notes of what you observe and write everything down in your journal when you get back to shore. Remember to record the water temperature, cloud cover, and other changing environmental factors that may affect animal activity.

Bottom Viewer:
Using a Movable Observatory

Using a mask and snorkel works well in the summer when the water is warm, but what if you want to see what's going on below the lake's surface at other times of the year? To peek at the creatures in a lake or pond when the water is cold, you can build a portable bottom viewer using the instructions in the Appendix at the back of this book. A bottom viewer is a great tool for investigating pond and lake life, and it helps eliminate the glare caused by the sun reflecting off the water's surface.

When you're ready to test out your bottom viewer, grab some waders, a collecting jar or sampling pan, an aquatic net, and a magnifying lens, and head to a nearby lake or pond. Select a site where you can safely wade into the water. Place the bottom viewer a little below the water's surface and look down into the water.

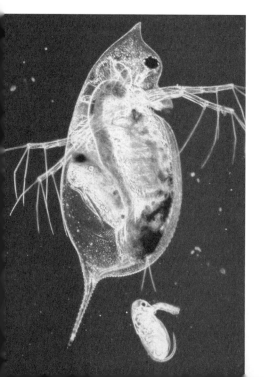

An adult and young Daphnia

It might take a few moments for your eyes to focus. Once they have adjusted, you should be able to see all kinds of interesting organisms. Moving your bottom viewer about in the water might send some of the living things into hiding, so try to move it slowly and let the surrounding area settle before you begin your observations.

Look for insects, worms, fishes, **amphibians,** and **crustaceans,** including *Daphnia*. *Daphnia* are about the size of a pinhead and are easily identified by their jerky swimming style. They are an important source of food for fish. Record the organisms you see in your journal.

————————————————————⁓⁓⁓⁓⁓⁓⁓⁓⁓⁓

What Are You?
Identifying the Creatures You Find

As you explore the many habitats of lakes and ponds, you will find a wide variety of animals, including insects. Many of them will be completely new to you and learning their identities will involve a little detective work. You'll also need to learn how to use a **key**—a guide that has pictures and descriptions to help you figure out the names of organisms. At first, the job of identifying creatures might seem overwhelming, but the more you use a key, the more comfortable you'll become with it.

The easiest keys to use are based on drawings or photographs of animals. The illustrations may have arrows pointing to the notable characteristics and features of each animal. Field guides to birds, mammals, reptiles and amphibians, and fishes are easy to find in most libraries and bookstores.

To identify insects and other invertebrates, such as those shown in Figure 7 on the next page, you'll need to learn how to use a **dichotomous** key. But first, you'll have to learn some **morphological** terms for the group of organisms you are trying to identify. Some common terms used to describe insects are given in Figure 8 on page 37.

A dichotomous key is arranged in couplets. Each couplet gives two possible descriptions of an organism. From each couplet, pick the description that best fits the organism you are trying to identify. At the end of each description, a number refers you on to a new couplet. Go to that couplet and again choose the description that fits your organism. By working your way through the key, you narrow down the choices until you arrive at the name of the organism. The number of paired choices you

Figure 7 Some Common Lake and Pond Insects

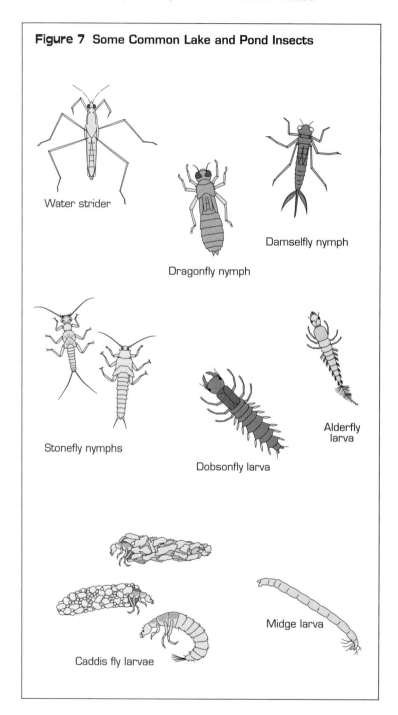

Water strider

Dragonfly nymph

Damselfly nymph

Stonefly nymphs

Dobsonfly larva

Alderfly larva

Caddis fly larvae

Midge larva

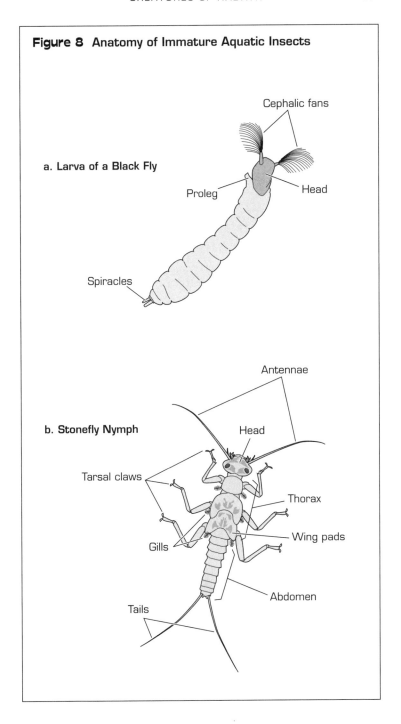

Figure 8 Anatomy of Immature Aquatic Insects

Cephalic fans

a. Larva of a Black Fly

Proleg

Head

Spiracles

Antennae

b. Stonefly Nymph

Head

Tarsal claws

Thorax

Wing pads

Gills

Abdomen

Tails

may have to go through to identify the mystery organism can vary.

Follow these commonsense rules as you work through a key:

- Read through each choice carefully and completely, even if the first statement seems to be the right one. You may find that the second statement is an even better description of the specimen.
- If measurements are given in the key, measure your specimen. Don't guess.
- Where technical terms are given, look up the exact meaning in the glossary or another reference if you are not sure.
- Don't base your conclusions on only one part of a specimen, or even on a single specimen. There is always variation between different individuals, and the single specimen you are trying to identify might be atypical.

Using a Dichotomous Key

The dichotomous key for immature aquatic insects shown in Figure 9 is adapted from one created by aquatic biologist J. G. Needham. Try working an insect you find through this key. For example, if you caught a stonefly like the one shown in Figure 8 on page 37, you would pick the first description given in Couplet 1 of the key—your insect has visible wings. Choosing that description sends you to Couplet 2 of the key.

It might be difficult to tell whether your specimen has biting mouthparts or not, but with a magnifying glass or hand lens, you should be able to rule out the second choice—whether or not the insect has a jointed sucking beak. Choosing the first description in Couplet 2 sends you to Couplet 3.

Here, the choice is pretty clear—your insect has long, slender tails, and it doesn't have a labium—a part of the

Figure 9   Key to the Orders of Aquatic Insects

1. Larvae with wings developing externally ... **2**
   Larvae with wings developing internally (invisible until the pupal stage); wormlike ... **5**

2. With biting mouthparts ... **3**
   Mouth parts combined into a jointed sucking beak ... **Water bugs**

3. With long slender tails; labium not longer than the head, and folded on itself like a hinge ... **4**
   With tails represented by three broad, leaflike gills or small appendages; labium longer than the head when extended; folds like a hinge ... **Damselflies and dragonflies**

4. With gills mainly under the thorax; two tarsal claws; two tails ... **Stoneflies**
   Gills mainly on the sides of the abdomen; generally three tails ... **Mayflies**

5. With jointed thoracic legs ... **6**
   Without jointed thoracic legs; with abdominal prolegs, or entirely legless ... **Flies**

6. With slender, piercing mouthparts, head as long as the body; small larvae, living on fresh water sponges ... **Neuroptera**
   With biting mouthparts ... **7**

7. With a pair of prolegs on the last segment only; these are directed backward, and each is armed with one or two strong hooks or claws ... **8**
   With prolegs, when present, on more than one abdominal segment; if present on the last segment, then not armed with single or double claws ... **9**

8. With abdominal segments, each with a pair of long, lateral filaments ... **Neuroptera**
   With abdominal segments without long, muscular, lateral filaments, often with minute gill filaments; cylindrical larvae, generally living in portable cases. ... **Caddis flies**

9. With five pairs of prolegs, and no spiracles at the bottom of the abdomen ... **Moths**
   Usually without prolegs; never with five pairs; usually with terminal spiracles; long filaments sometimes present on the abdominal segments ... **Beetles**

mouth—that is longer than its head. Choosing the first description sends you on to Couplet 4 of the key. Here again the choice is clear. Your specimen has two tails, or **cerci.** This line leads you to the name of the organism—it's a stonefly.

It is useful to study a dichotomous key before you start using it. What are the critical features the key asks you to look for and make choices about? What are some commonly used technical terms that you are not familiar with?

Once you key your specimen to the proper group, find a more specific key and use it to further identify the specimen.

Striding on the Water's Surface

Water molecules are made up of one oxygen atom and two hydrogen atoms. They are strongly attracted to one another because of the way the atoms are arranged in the molecule. At the interface of the water's surface and the air, the attraction between the water molecules is particularly strong. This physical property is called **surface tension.**

To investigate the properties of the water's surface, you'll need waxed paper, some toothpicks, dish-washing detergent, a shallow pan, and a drinking glass.

Sprinkle some water drops on a 15-centimeter (6-in.) square of waxed paper. Notice how the drops bead up. The smallest drops are nearly round, and the larger ones are slightly flattened. Use a toothpick to move the drops around so they combine with one another. Describe the differences in the shapes of the combined droplets. What do you think accounts for the fact that the drops stay together?

Next put a little bit of dish-washing detergent on the end of a toothpick. Touch the water droplets with the detergent-coated toothpick. What happens to the water drops? What do you think causes this? If you said that the detergent lessened the attraction of the surface molecules, you are right.

Now put some water in a shallow pan. Sprinkle a little baby powder over the water's surface. What happens? Repeat the experiment, but this time put a drop of dish-washing detergent in the center of the water. Can you explain what you see? Is there a relationship between what you observed with the water drops and what you observed with the pan of water?

Next, fill a clear drinking glass half full of water. Look at the glass from the side. Does the surface look the same as the rest of the water in the glass?

Surface tension can be quite strong. It can even support a needle carefully laid upon the surface. Surface tension allows some creatures to live on the water's surface. When certain substances are added to the water, such as soap or detergent, the surface tension is weakened and the surface is more easily penetrated.

Now, collect some insects from your lake or pond using an aquatic net (see the Appendix for instructions on constructing a net). Toss some of the insects onto the surface of the water in a lake, pond, or aquarium. What happens to most of them? Some may become trapped by the surface tension as the water clings to their bodies. Do larger insects have more trouble freeing themselves than smaller ones? Insects that get themselves trapped in the surface film become a food supply for a variety of aquatic creatures. If you do this experiment in a lake or pond, look for the spreading ripples where fish have risen to the surface to grab a struggling insect.

On lakes and ponds around the world you are likely to find insects called water striders. These insects have hairs at the end of their feet that spread their weight so they can glide over the surface of the water and not get trapped in the surface film.

Collect several water striders with a net—it's easier said than done. They are fast and have piercing mouthparts that can stick you, so be careful. Release the insects into a shallow plastic pan, preferably white, and put the pan where the sun or artificial light will create shadows on the bottom. Look closely at the insects' shadows. Do you see round circles at the end of their legs? Toss a fly, or mosquito, or other small insect into the pan. How does its shadow differ from that of a water strider? Leave the pan undisturbed for a while. How do the water striders interact with the other insects you dropped on the surface?

✔ Doing More

You should now be ready to investigate water striders in the wild. As you observe their behavior, ask yourself the following questions:

- Do water striders ever go beneath the surface?
- Do you see them feeding?
- Do the water striders interact with each other?
- Can you tell young water striders from adult ones?
- Where do water striders lay their eggs?

Life at the Top:
More Creatures on the Water

What other creatures dwell on the water's surface? Do you see any shiny black beetles gyrating on the surface? These are whirligig beetles. They interact with one another by sending out ripples as they swim. Notice how they occasionally dive below the surface. How do you think they breathe when they dive? (Hint: Look for a shiny air bubble on their undersides.) What adaptations do these beetles have that allow them to function as well on the surface as below it? (Hint: Check out their divided eyes.)

Most aquatic insects that lack gills breathe in their oxygen from the air. The trick is to get the oxygen they need without becoming the prey of birds, frogs, and other creatures. Mosquito larvae, giant water bugs, and water scorpions have all developed a unique adaptation for

A whirligig beetle can stand on the water's surface.

solving this problem. They have a breathing tube that they can poke above the water's surface. These creatures can use their tubes to take in oxygen from the air while remaining safely below the water's surface. Can you find these snorkel-like structures on the animals you observe?

Warm, shallow water around the edges of lakes and ponds cannot hold as much dissolved oxygen as cooler, deeper waters can. That is why most of the insects found close to shore get their oxygen from the air rather from the water. Check the insects you come across for the presence or absence of gills. Gills can be located on different parts of the insect's body, but they are all feathery in appearance. Do any of the gilled creatures live near the surface? Are any of the non-gilled creatures regularly found well below the surface? If so, how do they carry air when they dive? You may have to examine the creatures closely with a hand lens to find out.

Midwater Creatures: It's Their Density

In midwater, you will discover a variety of creatures that are active swimmers. Some, such as *Daphnia*, copepods, and the miniature clamlike ostracods, are very tiny. Others, such as water boatmen are much larger. And of course there are fish as well as frogs and newts. All these organisms have solved a similar problem: How to regulate their body density so they don't sink to the bottom or bob back up to the surface. Try to determine how each creature solves this problem. What adaptations do they have to help them? You might notice that the organisms have a variety of paddle and fin shapes that help them move through the water. But what keeps them suspended in midwater?

If you go swimming and try to dive down deep you will most likely have some trouble. Your body will tend to float upward if you don't keep paddling your way downward. That's because most people's bodies are less dense than water. The laws of buoyancy, which describe the force that keeps certain objects from sinking, push you up toward the surface. However, a few people, particularly boys with very low body fat, are denser than water and tend to sink rather than float. If you are a floater, a belt with some diver's weights attached will help you sink. By choosing the right amount of weight, you can achieve the same density as the water and remain suspended.

If you dissect a fish, you will notice a balloonlike bladder in the fish's body (see Figure 10 on page 45). This bladder removes air from the fish's blood and stores it.

Note the two egg sacs clinging to the tail segments of each of these copepods

The more air in the bladder, the less dense the fish's body and the more likely it is to float upward. If some of the air is released from the bladder, the fish will sink. Fish can regulate the air in their bladder so that they remain suspended. If a fish's bladder is damaged, it loses its ability to stay suspended and probably won't live long.

Other midwater swimmers have various ways of adjusting their density. Some insects that dive with a bubble of air for breathing must keep paddling, or they will be pushed up to the surface. As they use up their air bubble, their density changes. Then they don't have to swim

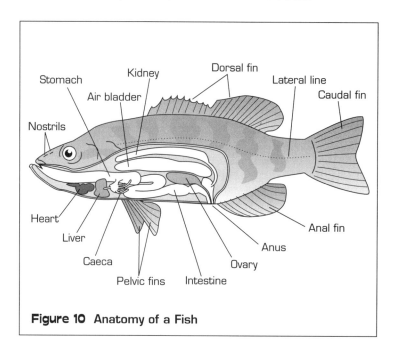

Figure 10 Anatomy of a Fish

as hard to stay suspended, but soon they'll have to return to the surface for a new air supply.

INVESTIGATION **3**

Caught in the Middle: Examining the Plankton

To see what kinds of creatures might be hanging out in the midwaters of your lake or pond, you'll need to catch some in a **plankton** net (see the Appendix for instructions on constructing your own net). You'll also need a container to hold your catch, some rubbing alcohol to preserve the creatures you catch for future examination, a light microscope, a medicine dropper or pipette, and some microscope slides and coverslips.

If you have access to a rowboat or canoe, you can row or paddle around the lake or pond and try to net some plankton samples at various water depths. Or you can just wade into the water to collect your sample. Sweep the plankton net through the water at least 30 centimeters (12 in.) below the surface. While the net is still underwater, close off the opening with your free hand so that you don't pick up any creatures from the water's surface. Pull the net out of the water and dump the contents into your container.

Before you examine your catch under the microscope, swirl the contents of the jar around in case things have settled to the bottom. Using the dropper, place a few drops of your sample on a microscope slide and affix the coverslip. In your journal, draw what you see, and use a key to aquatic invertebrates to help you identify what you have found (see the For Further Information section for the names of some keys).

Bottom Dwellers
and Plant Dwellers

Some creatures spend most of their lives crawling across the bottom of a lake or pond or hanging onto the stems of plants. Most of these insects swim quite awkwardly, if at all. Almost all of them take in dissolved oxygen through gills. A few, including some kinds of mosquitoes, get oxygen by extracting it from the stems of aquatic plants.

Other creatures, such as pill clams and mussels, burrow into the soft mud at the bottom. As you snorkel around a lake or pond near your home, look for their **siphons** protruding into the water and sucking in small organisms that pass by. Can you take a guess at what they eat? The siphons pull the food into the animal's body and send water out.

While you're swimming around, look out for leeches. These segmented worms move through the water by undulating their bodies in a wavelike motion. They do this by alternately compressing and releasing body fluids.

This snail and its young slide along a trail of mucus that the adult lays down.

This action pushes the worm through the water. When a leech finds a turtle, fish, or other potential food, it grasps hold of the creature with its suckerlike mouth and bores a hole through the skin in search of blood. When the leech is full of blood, it releases its grip and undulates away to hide while it digests its meal.

Look on the bottom or on plant stems for snails glid-ing along a trail of the mucus that they secrete. This mucus allows them to move over all kinds of surfaces, including the surface film of the water. They get the nutrients they need to survive by scraping algae and dead plant cells off of rocks or the bottom.

Bottom Dwellers at Work

To find out how clams get their food from the water around them, try this experiment. You'll need some food coloring, a small bowl of water, and a medicine dropper or pipette.

Add some food coloring to the bowl of water. Draw up some of the colored water into a medicine dropper or pipette. Put the dropper and its colored water into the pond near the siphons and release the dye slowly. (You can also dig up some clams and "replant" them in an aquarium to do this investigation.) As you release the dye, watch how the siphons create a current of water that pulls the dye into one siphon and expels it from the other. Tadpoles also use a siphoning system to take in food, but they expel the water through their gills. If you have access to some tadpoles, you can use the dye and dropper technique to observe how they feed.

Some other interesting bottom creatures to observe are dragonfly nymphs (or **naiads**). You are probably more familiar with the fast-flying adult dragonflies that cruise over the water searching for flying insects to eat or engaging in their mating rituals. The naiads stalk along the bottom of lakes and ponds in search of food. If you spot one during your observations, watch it carefully—you may see it feed. Smaller dragonfly species eat aquatic insects, while larger ones, such as the common green darner, eat tadpoles and small fish as well as aquatic insects.

Folded over the immature insect's face is a mask-like structure. Look closely and you will see that this is attached to leglike structures below the head. When the dragonfly larvae is close to its prey the "legs" and "mask" unfold and dart forward to grasp the prey. The prey is then pulled back to the

In this photo of a dragonfly nymph lying on its back, you can see the insect's spoon-shaped labia.

dragonfly's head where it is devoured by powerful jaws hidden beneath the mask.

There are many kinds of dragonflies in North America. Some prefer ponds; others prefer streams. If you observe adult dragonflies around you, you will probably get a chance to see the naiads. Look for them crawling about on the bottom or lying in the mud, half hidden from view, as they wait for food to pass close enough to grab.

Building a Reference Collection

This project involves making a collection of aquatic creatures in your lake or pond. You will need glass or clear plastic vials with caps or some empty baby-food jars with lids, a shallow white tray, strips of paper for labels, rubbing alcohol to preserve the specimens, and a dark lead pencil. (Unlike ink, pencil marks will not run or dissolve when you put alcohol into the vials.)

Out in the lake or pond, use your plankton net or larger aquatic net (see Appendix for instructions on making these) to scoop up some organisms. Place each specimen you collect into a vial or jar filled with alcohol. You can put more than one specimen of the same organism in each jar or vial. For each kind of organism collected and preserved, put as much information on the label as you can. You should include the name of the organism, the date you collected it, and the place you found it. It is usually best to put the label inside the vial rather than on the outside so that it does not peel off and get lost.

Fill out the label so that you can identify each creature as accurately as possible. (Refer back to Project 2 for help in identifying your specimens.) You may not be able to determine the species name for all the organisms you find. However, you can determine that later, perhaps with the help of an **entomologist.**

Try to include a wide range of aquatic insects as well as crustaceans, small fishes, and aquatic worms in your reference collection. You can include some algae and plant samples too.

You can build this reference collection over a long period of time. Making a reference collection will help you become more familiar with the range of creatures that live in the lake or pond you are studying.

What Do Fish Eat? Examining the Catch

Many of the aquatic insects in the reference collection you created in Project 3 are the prey of fishes. To find out which fish eat which insects, crustaceans, and worms, you can examine the contents of their stomachs. For this project you'll need some fish or fish stomachs, some vials or baby-food jars, rubbing alcohol, some shallow white pans, a dissecting kit, and a magnifying lens.

To get some fish stomachs, you can catch some fish yourself or you can ask some local fishers to give you the stomachs of the fish they catch. If you catch the fish yourself, you'll need to find and remove their stomachs. Figure 10 on page 46 will help you do this. Once you have the stomachs, carefully slice them open and empty the stomach contents into a jar containing alcohol. Be sure the jar is labeled and closed tightly if you aren't going to examine the contents right away.

If you'd rather not kill a fish to see what is in its stomach, try using a fish-stomach pump to flush out the contents of the stomach. To make a fish-stomach pump you'll need a shallow pan, a spray bottle with a squeeze handle and an adjustable nozzle, some aquarium tubing measuring 10 to 15 centimeters (4 to 6 in.), a medicine dropper, and a pair of white cotton gloves (see Figure 11).

Use the pump on fishes that are at least 20 centimeters (8 in.) long. You'll also need a friend or fellow student to help you. Fill the spray bottle with water and place one end of the plastic tubing over the nozzle of the bottle (you may have to remove the cap from the nozzle to make the tubing fit). Remove the bulb of the medicine dropper.

Wearing the gloves, grasp the fish and hold its mouth over a shallow tray. Have a friend push the medicine dropper and tubing through the fish's mouth and into the digestive tract. Squeeze the handle of the bottle to flush the stomach contents into the shallow pan.

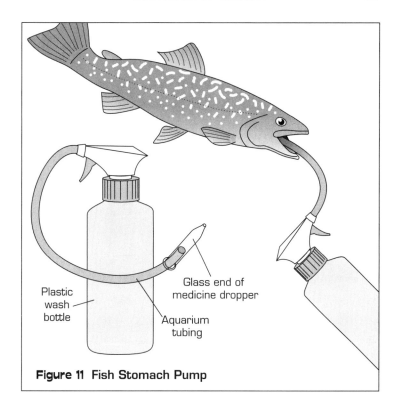

Figure 11 Fish Stomach Pump

Place the stomach contents in a jar of alcohol. Keep the stomach contents of only one species in each jar, and be sure to label each jar with the name of the fish species.

When you are ready to analyze the foods of a given species, spread out the stomach contents in a clean white pan. Use a dissecting needle to move materials around for better viewing, and a magnifying lens to enlarge your view of various parts. Sort the samples into categories of food, such as plants, insects, and small fish. Use species names whenever possible.

To help you identify partially digested organisms, compare them to your reference material. This kind of detective work takes patience. As time passes, you will recognize more of the material without having to constantly refer back to the reference collection. Keep a record of the number of creature parts you find. With this information you will be able to build a **food web** for the lake or pond your fish came from.

You also need to note the time of year when the stomach contents were collected. Food availability and preferences change with the seasons, and you can discover these seasonal changes through your stomach-analysis studies. Total the number of stomachs of a particular species in which each food item appeared. Divide the number of stomachs containing a particular food item by the total number of stomachs you examined. This will give you a percentage frequency of that item in the diet of that fish species at that time of year. For example:

Total number of fish stomachs containing
beetle wings = 15

Total number of fish stomachs examined = 20

$\frac{15}{20}$ = 0.75 × 100 = 75 percent of the fish stomachs
examined contained beetle wings

You can also figure out what percentage of a fish's diet is made up of a particular organism. Total the number of one type of organism you find, such as mayflies. Divide that number by the total number of organisms you find in the fish's stomach. Multiply the result by 100 to get a percentage. For example:

Number of mayflies found in fish stomach 1 = 4

Total number of insects found in fish stomach 1 = 24

$\frac{4}{24}$ = 0.166 × 100 = 16 percent of this fish's insect
diet consists of mayflies

✔ Doing More

The information you gathered will give you a rough estimate of the food habits of the fish you caught. Measuring the dry weight of all the food materials you collect, including plants and algae, will give you a wider view of the food habits of the fish. Record the data you collect as shown Table 1. You can photocopy the table or redraw it in your journal.

Table 1 Fish Stomach Contents			
Organism Found	Number of Individuals Found	Weight	Percent of Total Weight
Mayfly	4	0.005 g	20 percent
Stonefly	2	0.005 g	20 percent
Caddis fly	4	0.005 g	20 percent

Turtle Watching

Almost every lake and pond has turtles. You will often spot them sunning themselves on logs. You may also occasionally see their heads popping above the surface of the water among aquatic plants. Do the same turtles always sun on the same rock or log? Do turtles move to different spots in the lake or pond at different seasons? To answer these questions, you need to be able to identify individual turtles. This isn't as impossible as it sounds. After you observe for a while, you'll start to notice individual variations in the turtles you see. Maybe one is a slightly different color or has some other identifying sign. Did a narrow escape from a predator leave a mark on the shell, for example? Watch the turtles in a lake

Florida cooters are found in lakes and ponds in the southern United States.

or pond for several months and keep track of their activities. This will help you understand what life is like for a turtle.

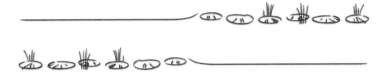

How Are Waterbirds Adapted for Their Lives?

Of course you can watch waterbirds with your naked eye, but for serious observing, it helps to have a pair of binoculars. Look for long-legged waders such as egrets or herons patrolling the shoreline. How does the length of their legs affect their position in the water? Do shorter-legged green herons feed in different places than great blue herons or sandhill cranes? Herons have to be able to see their food beneath the surface. What behaviors help the birds avoid reflections

As a great blue heron wades along the shore, it uses its long neck and spearlike bill to grab fish.

of sunlight on the water? These physical and behavioral adaptations help waterbirds get food in their chosen habitat.

Scientists use the word **niche** to describe the role an organism plays in its environment. What an organism eats, where it lives, and how its activities affect the non-living aspects of its surroundings are all part of its niche. Different creatures, even closely related ones, occupy different niches in pond and lake environments. Their adaptations, physical and behavioral, help them live successfully. Try to determine the adaptations of every creature you observe—from the tiniest to the largest—and figure out its niche. The adaptations and niches of some creatures are quite obvious, but figuring out the niches of others takes much closer observation over a longer time period.

Ducks, geese, and swans occupy a variety of niches in aquatic environments. They are relatively easy to observe and have some adaptations that are easy to spot. Which of these birds has feet located toward the rear of its body? This placement lets the birds dive more easily and push themselves through the water more smoothly, but it also makes them awkward on land.

The legs of other waterbirds are closer to the middle of their body. When these birds put their heads into the water to look for food, their whole body tips forward and their legs and feet may stick up out of the water. These species have to feed in shallow water or on creatures near the surface. How are the bills of different birds adapted for the food they eat? Can you spot serrated edges along their bills? These edges make it easier for the birds to grab slippery fish. Which species are more often found on ponds than on lakes? What adaptations make them more suited to one body of water or the other?

Record your observations in your journal. Read your journal from time to time to look for patterns between environmental factors such as the weather, or the temperature, and the behaviors of the creatures you observe. Be sure to write down any questions you might have about what you see. As you look over your journal, you may discover the answer to an earlier question.

Out in the Cold:
Lakes and Ponds in Winter

A variety of organisms remain active in winter, mainly birds, mammals, some fishes, and some aquatic insects and crustaceans. It can be exciting to discover which of the creatures in your lake or pond are active in the cold weather. How have they adapted to the difficulties and opportunities of the winter environment?

Winter Duck Watch

From late fall to early spring, ducks congregate wherever there is open water on lakes and ponds—often near the inlet or outfall of the body of water. As winter approaches, most species begin courting and establishing pair bonds. Their antics are both amusing and instructive. A bird identification guide will help you determine what kind of ducks you are watching.

Choose an individual duck and follow its behavior for a period of time. Record all the things you see it do: swim quietly, rest with its head under its wing, tip tail-up and head-down in the water, preen, bob its head up and down, or interact with other ducks. Pay particular attention to what happens when

The hen, or female, pintail duke is on the left. The drake, or male, is on the right.

two or more ducks appear to "meet." Sometimes, having a friend or classmate observing with you helps to keep things straight. As soon as the duck you are watching begins to interact with another duck, ask your friend to follow the activity of the second duck. In time, you will be able to predict the ducks' behavior.

In mallards, you will see such behaviors as the grunt whistle, bobbing motions, birds swimming with their heads and tails up, and birds swimming along nodding their heads. The birds use these behaviors to communicate their feelings to other birds of the same species. Early in the season, many behaviors indicate aggression—the birds are saying, "Go away and leave me alone!"

As the winter progresses, more and more birds will find a mate. Their behaviors will become less aggressive and more directed toward strengthening their bond with a bird of the opposite sex. By the end of winter, most of the birds will have found a mate, and you will recognize the pairs. However, there will still be some aggressive behavior as bachelor males try to break up pairs and take the females for themselves. Be sure to record your observations and questions in your journal.

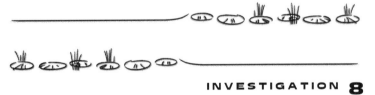

Signs in the Snow

Ice turns the surface of lakes and ponds into traffic lanes for a number of creatures that are active in winter. Look for the tracks of animals and birds in the snow covering the ice. Be careful in your explorations—always make sure the ice is thick enough for you to walk on. Remember, the ice gets thinner where streams leave or enter a lake or pond. Be especially cautious if you hear gurgling water. The ice might also be thin near the entrances of beaver lodges.

Beavers tend to stay in their lodges underneath the ice in the winter, but occasionally they may venture out. Beaver

Beavers are responsible for forming many new ponds.

tracks are about 8 to 13 centimeters (3 to 5 in.) long. They might be difficult to make out because beavers drag their wide tails behind them and may brush over the tracks. Be on the lookout for the tracks of minks and otters as they hunt for food such as crayfish, mussels, tadpoles, and fish beneath the ice. If you come across animal tracks, follow them and try to re-create the activity of the animals. Where did they stop to check out the surroundings? Where did they "answer nature's call"? Can you find any remains of feeding activity, such as bones or feathers? Do you find evidence of one animal interacting with others?

CHAPTER 3

Meet the Greens: The Plant Life in Lakes and Ponds

BELOW THE SURFACE OF LAKES AND ponds lies a largely unexplored world of aquatic plants. Plants are a vital component of lakes and ponds. They provide food and a place to live for many lake and pond animals, and if they are growing underwater, they add oxygen to the water.

During photosynthesis, plants combine sunlight, carbon dioxide, and water to form simple sugars and oxygen. Remember that even though they might be living in water, all animals need some form of oxygen to survive. Plants use oxygen too. When the sun goes down, plants switch from photosynthesis to **respiration.** As in animals, plants respire to get energy by combining oxygen and sugars. Respiration releases carbon dioxide, which can be used for photosynthesis when the sun come up.

A few species of aquatic plants float and flower at the surface. Their fine roots hang into the water where they can pull in dissolved minerals and gases. These include duckweed and water meal. These plants are capable of rapid reproduction by dividing their leaves to form new plants. Sometimes the plants double in number every few days until they completely cover a pond's surface.

The best-known watcr plants are **water-tolerant plants**—or emergent plants. They can tolerate having their roots and stems in the water, but need to have their leaves out in the air. This group of plants includes cattails, arrowhead, pickerelweed, and water lilies. These plants are generally found in shallow water along the edges of lakes and ponds.

The **submergent plants,** the lesser-known plants of ponds and lakes, are totally submerged except for their

Pickerelweed is a common emergent plant found in marshes and along the edges of ponds.

flowering parts. The leaves of these true aquatics are often long and thin to maximize their contact with the water. Some have broader leaves, but they too are very thin.

On the Edge:
Exploring the Emergent Zone

Emergent plants are the easiest to study because they seldom grow in water that is more than chest deep. Native Americans found that the edges of ponds and streams are a storehouse of nutritious plant foods. Cattails are a versatile food plant. In spring, the young stems can be peeled and used in salads. The first shoots can be cooked like asparagus, and the roots can be cooked and eaten like potatoes! You can even make flour from the dried roots and pollen.

The starchy seeds of pickerelweed can be eaten raw or dried and used as a cereal, or dried and ground into flour. The tender young leaves can be used like spinach. A number of other pond-edge plants, including water shield, wild calla, and water lily, also have nutritious greens and starchy roots. Among the best-tasting potato-like plants are arrowheads and duck-potatoes. The tubers that grow at the ends of the long runners that originate from the base of each plant are a favorite of many aquatic animals and people. The runners help the plants spread across the pond bottom.

Emergent plants make good homes for a variety of animals. Several species of frogs, ribbon and water snakes, turtles, muskrats, red-winged blackbirds, dragonflies, and damselflies are among the animals you are likely to find living in the emergent zone. These plant communities are often nurseries for fish too. Here, young fishes find shelter from the larger fishes that prey on them. Fish are the most obvious creatures in emergent plant communities, but if you study the community more closely, you will find snails and snail eggs, aquatic insects, and many other small creatures.

Red-winged blackbirds are frequently found along the shores of lakes and ponds.

The flowers of emergent plants are often unusual, ranging from the fuzzy spikes of cattails to the strange hooded flowers of arums. White water lilies have truly beautiful flowers, as do their cousins, the lotuses. An emergent shrub called buttonbush has ball-shaped clusters of flowers. Pickerelweed has spikes of blue-purple flowers that brighten the water's edge with beautiful patches of color.

INVESTIGATION 9

Measuring Light Using a Secchi Disk

Plants and algae need light to grow. Because water and the materials suspended in it absorb light, the amount of light in a lake or pond decreases as the water depth increases or as the amount of material suspended in the water increases. The amount of light determines where plants can grow in a lake or pond.

Scientists use a light meter to measure the amount of light available at different depths. You can make similar measurements using a simple black-and-white disk called a Secchi disk—named for its inventor, an eighteenth-century Italian oceanographer (see Appendix for instructions on making a Secchi disk).

Take a Secchi disk and two spring-loaded clothespins to your lake or pond. From the dock, or over the side of a boat, slowly lower the disk into the water and watch it descend. It's easier to see the disk if you work from the shaded side of the boat or under a shade tree. Mark the depth at which you can no longer see the disk by clipping a clothespin to the rope. Lower the disk a few inches, and then begin to raise it slowly. Mark the rope again when the Secchi disk reappears. Add these two depths together and divide the result by two to get an average Secchi-depth reading for that spot.

The reading is the deepest point at which enough light reflects off the disk for you to see. Most readings will be in the neighborhood of 6 to 30 feet. Even though you might not be able to see the disk, some light still gets through the water. For a rough approximation of the lowest depth at which plants receive enough light to survive, multiply your Secchi depth reading by two.

✔ Doing More
Use your Secchi disk to record the changes in light penetration in your lake or pond throughout the year. Is the light penetration the same in the spring and fall? What would an algae bloom do to your readings?

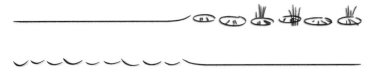

It's a Matter of Depth
To find out where specific plants like to grow in a lake or pond, you'll need to create a **transect line**—a straight line along the plants—and record all the plants that touch the line (see Figure 12). To do this you'll need two poles (old broom handles work well), a yardstick, an indelible marker, ten bottle corks, and about 25 feet of cord. Cut the bottle corks into $\frac{1}{2}$ -inch

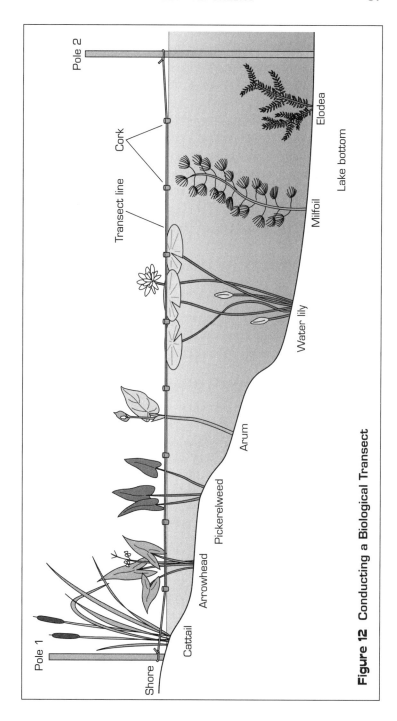

Figure 12 Conducting a Biological Transect

disks and drill a hole through the center of each. Feed the corks onto the cord before tying the cord to the poles. Ten cork disks are usually enough. The corks help the cord float when your line is set up. Tie the cord about 6 inches from the bottom of one pole and the same distance from the top of the other. Then, using the indelible marker, mark the cord every 12 inches.

Shape the ends of the poles into points so that they are easier to push into the lake bottom. Push the pole with the cord 6 inches from the bottom into the pond or lake shore until the cord is at the water's surface. Wade out beyond the last emergents, unwinding the cord as you go, and push the other pole into the bottom so that the cord is at a right angle to the shore. Adjust the floats to help keep the cord visible.

Use a yardstick to measure the water depth at each mark along the cord. Record your data in your journal (see Table 2). Draw a sketch of the transect line and note the depth above each marker on the line. From this data you can prepare a chart showing a profile of the shoreline from the shore to the farther pole.

Go back and identify each of the plants along your transect line. Use one of the reference books on aquatic plants listed in the For Further Information section to help you identify what you find. Figure 13 illustrates some common plant terms that you will probably encounter in the reference books.

Table 2   Distribution of Aquatic Plants Along a Transect Line

Site	Plant Species	Distance from Shore	Material on Bottom	Water Depth	Relative Abundance
1	Bladderwort	1 foot	Mud	1.5 feet	10 plants
2	Cattails	Water's edge	Gravel	Water's edge	Approx. 45 plants

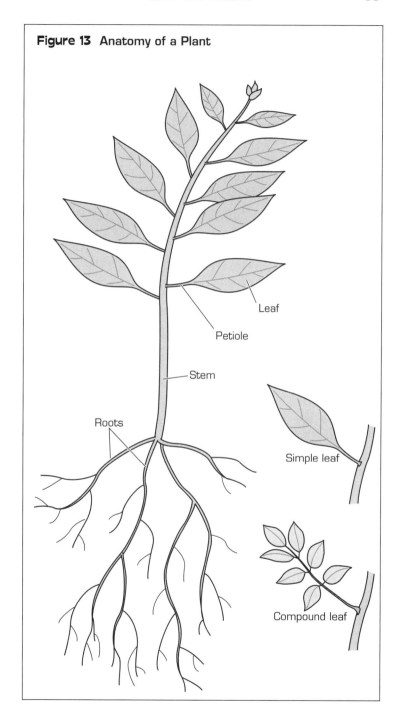

Figure 13 Anatomy of a Plant

Leaf

Petiole

Stem

Roots

Simple leaf

Compound leaf

Sketch the plants where they fall on your depth profile. Repeat the whole process in several places along the shoreline of the lake or pond you are studying.

Looking at the data you have gathered, can you determine the maximum and minimum depths at which each species grows? As you look at the plants in other places around the pond or lake, or even in another body of water, can you predict with some accuracy the depth at which they grow? You can check your predictions by running a transect line at the places where you made predictions.

INVESTIGATION 10

Finding Out About Submergent Plants

A number of pond and lake plants grow completely submerged in water. Only their flowering parts reach up to or above the water's surface. Those that are completely submerged at all times have very thin cell walls that make it easier for dissolved materials in the water to enter a plant's cells. The leaves are often finely divided so they have more surface area in contact with the water. This also makes it possible for the plants to absorb dissolved materials from the water more effectively. Submergent plants include bladderwort, water milfoil, hornwort, and *Elodea*. Most of these plants are found in the quiet waters where a current carries dissolved nutrients to them.

Collecting submergent plants is most easily done using a plant hook. (See the Appendix for details on how you can make one.) Throw the plant hook from shore or tow it behind a boat. Drag the hook over the bottom and haul in the plants you catch. Use a reference book on aquatic plants to help you identify the plants you pull in (see the For Further Information section). You can also use a snorkel and face mask to collect plants in water too deep for wading.

The Distribution of Aquatic Plants

Collect a few samples of each type of plant in your lake or pond. Note the depth range that each species seems to prefer as well as the type of bottom or **substrate**—gravelly, sandy, or muddy—that each plant prefers. Does the substrate change as you move out into the water?

Aquatic plants also serve as a growing surface for other creatures, many of them quite small. Some creatures merely attach themselves to the plant stems. Others use the plant for food as well as for shelter. Look closely at the stems. You may find creatures that look like a tiny stalk with a whorl of tentacles on top. These are *Hydra* (see Figure 14).

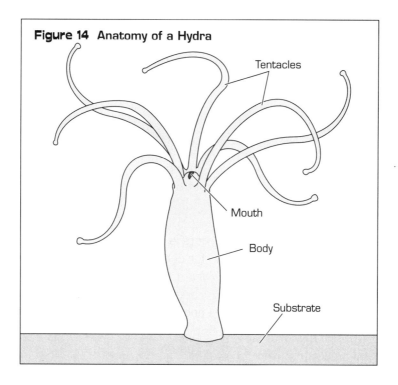

Figure 14 Anatomy of a Hydra

Tentacles

Mouth

Body

Substrate

〜〜〜〜〜〜〜〜〜〜〜〜─────────────

Setting Up a Home Observatory

Observing the creatures that make their homes on aquatic plants is best done by moving some of the plants into an aquarium filled with pond water. Aquariums come in a variety of sizes and types. Some are glass; others are plastic. Some are specifically designed to be aquariums, but you can use a number of plastic household storage containers as aquariums. Place some of the plants with *Hydra* on them into an aquarium along with some pond water.

Oxygen availability is important to keeping your organisms healthy. When selecting an aquarium, choose one with the largest water surface area relative to depth. If you get one that has a small surface area you will also need to purchase air stones and an aquarium pump to supply the necessary oxygen. Ask a person working at a pet store for advice on the best types of equipment for the aquarium you are setting up.

Tap water usually contains chlorine, which is toxic to many aquatic organisms. If possible, fill your aquarium with water from the pond or lake where you collected the plants. If this is not possible, put tap water in gallon jugs and let it sit uncovered for several days. The chlorine will escape from the water, and then it will be safe to use. You can also fill the aquarium with tap water and let it sit for a week before adding any organisms.

Give the plants and animals a day or two to adjust to their new environment. Place a piece of white paper behind the jar or aquarium to make it easier to see the organisms inside. Notice how some of the *Hydra* stay on the plant and others move onto the glass. How do they do this? Patient observation will reveal their interesting somersaulting movements.

You can also add some snails to your aquarium. Snails are often found on floating plants. They lay their eggs and feed on algae growing on the plant stems and leaves. How do these creatures move around? How do they scrape off the algae or cut into the plants themselves? Look on the underside of the front of the snail's foot for the mouth with circular rows of teeth called a **radula.** Be sure to keep detailed notes of changes in the aquarium and its inhabitants.

Use a medicine dropper to suck up some tiny aquatic creatures and examine them under a microscope. To make a slide for viewing, place a few drops of water on a microscope slide and cover it with a coverslip.

✔ Doing More

To keep things hopping, you can add some animals to your aquarium. Plastic tanks and household-storage boxes work well for studying aquatic insects and raising frogs, toads, and salamanders. Be sure to cover aquariums housing aquatic insects. You can use the covers that come with household storage boxes. Poke holes in these covers to let in air. Many aquariums can be covered with a mesh screen to keep creatures from jumping out.

A bullfrog lies in wait for a passing insect.

Identifying Aquatic Plants

Getting to know the many different plants and animals that live in lakes, ponds, and temporary pools can be challenging. Only a handful of them have common names and can be found in general field guides. To identify the rest, you will need to practice using dichotomous keys (see Project 2 on page 38). Once you get the hang of working with these keys, it is fairly easy to identify most of the organisms you find. The biggest challenge is to learn the technical vocabulary that is often used in such keys.

Choices on a dichotomous key build upon a variety of characteristics of the group of organisms you are investigating. For example, with plants you may be asked to make decisions about leaf shape, leaf margin, whether the leaf is simple or compound, the arrangement of the leaves on the stem, the presence of a **stipule**—a winglike or scalelike organ attached to the base of the leaf petiole or on the stem where the leaf attaches, the form of flowers, and the arrangement and location of flowers.

Using a key is like solving a puzzle. It can be fun, but it can also be frustrating. However, it is often the only way to identify the organism you are investigating. The technical terms for describing plant anatomy can be confusing. Most readily available keys have a glossary and diagrams that help explain the most frequently used terms.

Look in the For Further Information section at the back of this book for some keys that you might want to check out. For some, the publication dates may seem quite old, but don't worry. The information they contain is not likely to go out of date. Newer editions that sharpen the choices or bring the names up to date with recent revisions in the rules of classifying organisms (**taxonomy**) are published on a regular basis.

Bladderwort Trapping

Bladderworts are widely distributed aquatic, carnivorous plants. Carnivorous plants get their nitrogen supply by digesting insects and other animals that they trap. Generally, bladderworts float about a pond or lake. Their yellow blossoms reach above the water's surface. Along the plant's filamentous leaves are tiny sacs. When the sacs are empty, they tend to be flat. When a passing insect or crustacean bumps into them, they pop open, causing a sudden rush of water

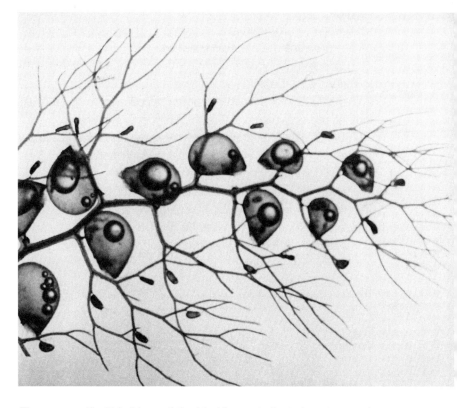

These magnified bladders of the bladderwort plant show trapped air bubbles and partially digested remains of trapped microscopic creatures.

Table 3   Bladderwort Trapping

Date and Time	Organism Found	Number of Individuals Found	Percent of Total Organisms
June 13, 10:45 A.M.	*Daphnia*	10	50 percent
June 14, 2:10 P.M.	Copepod	5	25 percent

that sucks in the animal. Once inside, the plant's chemicals begin to digest the trapped creature.

Collect some bladderwort plants and place them in a shallow white pan. Carefully examine each bladder on one or several plants. You'll probably need a microscope to get a close look at the organisms inside the bladders. Record your data in Table 3. You should also note the temperature and the pH of the water at the collecting site. (See Investigation 13 on page 86 for instructions on measuring pH.)

Make observations at different times of the day or night and record the time. Are the traps more successful at some times than at others? What do your bladderwort observations reveal about the overall ecology of the body of water where you found them?

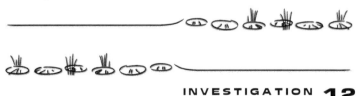

Cattail Architecture

Cattails are often found along the shores of many lakes and ponds. Notice that they always grow out in the open where they are fully exposed to the sunlight.

Cattails are commonly found along the shorelines of lakes and ponds.

Take a piece of paper or thin cardboard and cut a piece about the width and height of a cattail leaf. Hold it up by one end. Notice that the paper bends over and will not stay erect. How do you suppose the cattail, which has leaves of about the same thickness, is able to stay erect even in the wind? What is the tallest paper leaf you can make that will stay upright?

Examine a cattail leaf closely. Slit open a leaf and sketch what you see in your journal. Peel off the outer "skin" of the leaf. Again, draw what you see. How do these drawings compare with your paper leaf? The inner "ribbed" structure of the cattail leaf allows the plant to grow tall and get maximum exposure to sunlight for photosynthesis.

Examine the roots of several cattail plants. These plants store the food they make through photosynthesis in their roots. How do you think the architecture of the leaves contributes to the food-storage capacity of the plant? For many larger animals, cattail roots are an important winter food. What do you think the cattail's role is in the food chains and webs of the lake or pond where it grows?

Cattail leaves also help to reduce the energy of wind around the edges of lakes and ponds. As the wind bends each of the leaves in a stand of cattails, it gives up some of its energy. This helps make cattail stands a good place for animals to take shelter. What other roles do cattails play in the ecology of a pond or lake?

CHAPTER 4

A Place of Your Own: What Makes a Lake or Pond Unique?

EACH LAKE, POND, AND TEMPORARY pool is unique. Each has its own history, character, chemistry, plants, and animals. There are many similarities between bodies of water, but there are also significant differences.

The land surrounding a body of water largely determines the type and concentration of nutrients that flow into the water. The nutrients in turn affect the kinds of life that can become established in the water. The type of material on the lake or pond bottom—the substrate—determines the kinds of plants and bottom-dwelling creatures, or **benthic** organisms, that live there. The feeding habits of lake and pond inhabitants influence the numbers and types of other creatures you'll find there. Your challenge is to get to know the lake or pond you are exploring and to determine what is unique about it.

Why Is It Here?
The Location of a Lake or Pond

A map of a lake or pond can illustrate its unique landscape features. Among the most useful maps are the **topographic maps** available through the United States Geological Survey (see the For Further Information section for ordering information). These maps have **contour lines** that indicate a site's elevation above sea level.

The shape of these contour lines and the distance between them can tell you a lot about the landscape surrounding a body of water. If the distance between contour lines—the **contour interval**—is very small, the terrain there is very steep. If the lines are relatively far apart, the land slopes gradually. A topographic map also includes the outlines of bodies of water and shows where marshes or swamps border a lake or pond.

Lakes, ponds, and temporary pools collect water that flows down slopes. As the water moves down the incline, it erodes the land and dissolves minerals. Thus, the watershed surrounding a lake or pond contributes greatly to the character of the body of water. Water flowing down steep slopes brings more eroded material than water that flows down gradual slopes. Water seeping into the ground, rather than rapidly running off, contributes to the **groundwater** that may feed the lake or pond through natural springs.

PROJECT 9

Reading Contour Maps

Examine the contour map shown in Figure 15. What does the spacing of the lines indicate about the terrain? Can you

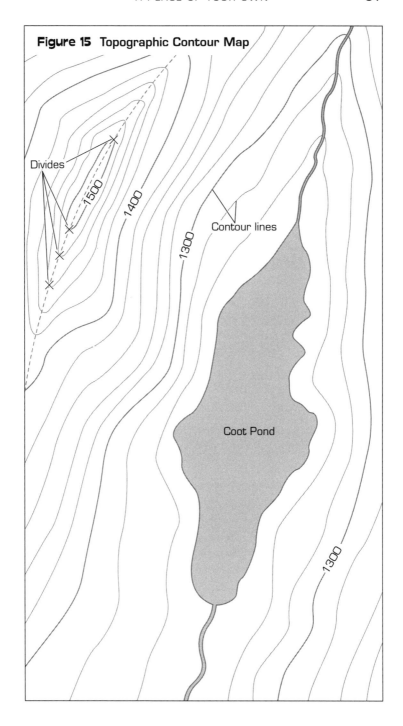

Figure 15 Topographic Contour Map

Divides

1500

1400

1300

Contour lines

Coot Pond

1300

plot the easiest walking route to the pond? On which edge of the pond would you expect to find the most gravel? Where would you expect the most silt and mud? Remember that water flowing over a steeper area flows faster and can carry larger particles of rock and sand. The heavier particles settle out faster once the flow slows down. Smaller particles are carried farther.

On the map, trace the contour lines out from the lake or pond until you reach the highest points surrounding the water. These points, called **divides,** mark the boundaries of the watershed. Water falling on the other side of a divide flows into a different watershed.

Get a topographic map that shows the lake or pond you are studying and look at it closely. Answer all the questions listed above. Draw a line from one divide to the next divide to show the borders of the watershed. What rivers and streams feed the lake or pond? Where do these waters flow? Are there any roads, houses, or industries within the watershed? How do you think these might affect the quality of water in your lake or pond? Are there other bodies of water in the same watershed? Are they linked to other lakes or ponds by feeder streams or groundwater?

Getting It on Paper: Mapping Your Site

The scale of topographic maps is often too large to be useful in your on-site investigations. They are best for getting a feel for the overall landscape in which your lake or pond is located. To record the places where you make specific discoveries, draw a map of the lake or pond. On it, you can mark the places where turtles regularly sun themselves, areas where sunfish make their nests, the locations of aquatic plants, and other interesting observations. The simplest way to make an accurate map of the body of water you are interested in is to photocopy the section of a topographic map that includes your pond or lake and then enlarge it several times until it is about the size of a sheet of notebook paper. Be sure to note the scale of the map you begin with and keep a record of each enlargement you make.

A common scale for topographic maps is 1 centimeter = 250 meters. On paper, your pond might be 10 centimeters long; this equals 2,500 meters. If you enlarge the map on the copy machine by 200 percent, the length of the pond will be 20 centimeters. The map would still represent 2,500 meters, but the scale of your map has changed—1 centimeter now represents 125 meters. You will need to keep this scale in mind when you measure things out at your pond.

PROJECT 10

Mapping the Shoreline

Depending on how large your lake or pond is, it might be difficult to make a map of the entire area. A more manageable project is to map a section of the shoreline using a transect line (see Figure 16 on the next page). You'll need a hammer, twelve stakes or poles, 120 meters (400 ft.) of rope, a 30-meter (100-foot) measuring tape, some flagging tape or strips of fabric, a permanent marker, and a waterproof pen or pencil.

Select a 100-meter (330-ft.) stretch of shoreline. On the bank, hammer a stake into the ground at each end of the stretch. Tie the rope from stake to stake to establish a baseline. Along the baseline, mark six or more stations at equally spaced intervals and number them with a marker. Run a rope, or transect, from each station out into the water. Each transect should be **perpendicular** to the baseline. The length of the transect line you run depends on how deep the water is.

You'll probably want to stay in water no more than 1 to 1.5 meters (3 to 4.5 ft.) deep. In the water, place another stake and attach the end of the rope to it. Using the mea-

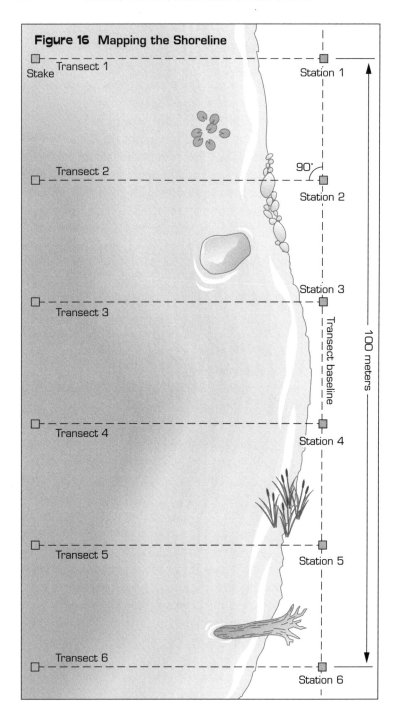

Figure 16 Mapping the Shoreline

Stake

Transect 1

Station 1

Transect 2

90°

Station 2

Station 3

Transect 3

Transect baseline

100 meters

Transect 4

Station 4

Transect 5

Station 5

Transect 6

Station 6

Table 4 Transect Line Data for Lake or Pond Mapping		
Transect	Feature	Distance from Station
1	Water's edge	3 meters (10 ft.)
1	Cattail stand	2 to 5 meters (6.5 to 16.4 ft.)

suring tape, measure the distance from the station to the features you would like to include on your map. You should record such features as the water's edge, large rocks, stands of aquatic plants, and any other interesting things you come across. Record the distances in your journal (see Table 4). Continue mapping by taking measurements at each station.

Once you've done all your measuring, it's time to make a map. You'll need a desk, paper, a ruler, and a pencil. Choose a map scale: try letting 1 centimeter on the map equal 5 meters (1 in. = 30 ft.). Draw the baseline to scale and mark and label the stations. Then draw in the transects. Mark the distances to the key landmarks you are including on your map. Connect the points that represent the same feature. For example, connect all the points that represent a stand of cattails.

✔ **Doing More**

As you work your way around the shoreline, you can combine the separate transect maps on the enlarged photocopy of a topographic map. When transferring the data, be sure to use the proper scale.

Something in the Water

Water that reaches a pond or lake in stream runoff or seeps in as groundwater carries a load of **organic** and **inorganic** material it has picked up along the way. The organic material—the remains of living things—includes such things as leaves and bacteria. Inorganic molecules, including minerals, comes from non-living sources, such as the rock over which the water flows. The amount and type of materials in the water can affect its physical characteristics, such as its pH and the amount of dissolved oxygen it can hold.

INVESTIGATION 13

Along the Scale: Measuring pH Levels

The pH of the water—its degree of acidity or alkalinity—is one of the tests used to measure the quality of water. pH is measured using a scale that goes from 0 to 14, with zero being the most **acidic** and 14 the most **basic.** The scale is a measure of the concentration of hydrogen ions (H^+) and hydroxide ions (OH^-) in the water. Water (H_2O) is a combination of these two ions. In its pure, distilled form, water has a pH of 7.0, right in the middle of the scale. As the concentration of H^+ ions increase, the water becomes more acidic. More OH^- ions mean the water is more basic.

Different forms of life prefer different pH levels (see Figure 17). Even closely related species might prefer very different pH levels. The pH of a pond or lake determines what kinds of organisms you might expect to find living there. Acidic waters, with a pH of 4.0 or lower, are usually lethal to most fish. Bass and bluegill seldom spawn in waters with a pH below 5.0, and their growth is slowed in waters between pH 5.0 and 6.5. Bass seem to do best in waters with a pH between 6.5 and 9.0.

An easy way to measure the pH of a body of water is with specially treated pH paper. You might be able to use some

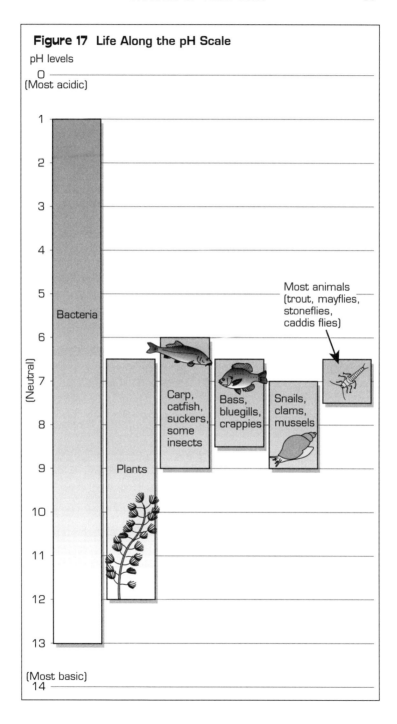

Figure 17 Life Along the pH Scale

pH levels

0 (Most acidic)

1

2

3

4

5

6 [Neutral]

Bacteria

Most animals (trout, mayflies, stoneflies, caddis flies)

Plants

Carp, catfish, suckers, some insects

Bass, bluegills, crappies

Snails, clams, mussels

7

8

9

10

11

12

13

14 (Most basic)

Table 5	Measuring pH Levels				
Site	Date	Time	pH	Organisms Observed
Clear Lake	August 10	11:00 A.M.	6.9	Bass

from your school science lab, or you can order some from a biological supply company (see the For Further Information section for the names and addresses). Collect some water from below the surface in a glass jar. Test your samples immediately upon collecting them because temperature changes can affect pH level. Record your data as shown in Table 5. You'll find that pH levels change throughout the year. Check the pH during a drought or after a heavy rainfall. Do you notice any differences?

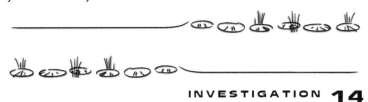

Measuring Dissolved Oxygen

Most aquatic plants and animals need some dissolved oxygen to survive, but the level needed varies greatly from organism to organism. The amount of dissolved oxygen in a body of water also indicates the general condition of a lake or pond. The greater the supply of dissolved oxygen, the greater the variety of life the water can sustain. When dissolved oxygen levels drop below about 4 milligrams per liter, warm-water fish such as pike and bass become stressed and may die.

A number of factors can cause the amount of dissolved oxygen in water to decrease. Warmer water holds less oxygen than colder water. Also, when dead plants and animals accumulate in lakes or ponds, they are consumed by bacteria and a variety of invertebrates. These creatures create a demand for oxygen and may quickly use up the supply in a lake or pond. That starts a vicious cycle in which more animals die and even more of the already scarce oxygen is used up. This decline in oxygen means that the diversity of living things in the water also declines.

Organic matter—in the form of decaying plants or animal wastes—can enter a pond or lake in a number of ways. Urban runoff enters through sewers. In rural areas, animal wastes may be washed into a stream and carried to a lake or pond. Animal waste can also find its way into lakes and ponds from food- and meat-processing plants. Organic matter might also be added by fallen leaves or dying aquatic plants. Either way, **aerobic** bacteria in the water use oxygen to break down these organic materials.

When the oxygen in the water is depleted, many kinds of aquatic insects die off. The entire food web of a lake or pond can be affected. Nuisance species of algae and **anaerobic** bacteria (those that can survive without oxygen) flourish.

The amount of dissolved oxygen in the water varies from day to night as the temperature changes and as photosynthesis comes to a halt with the diminishing sunlight. Plants and animals now begin to use oxygen through the process of respiration. The lowest oxygen levels usually occur just before dawn. When the sun comes up, plants start to photosynthesize again and release oxygen, which is a by-product of photosynthesis.

Testing for dissolved oxygen requires a little skill in chemistry. Measuring kits are pretty expensive so ask your science teacher if he or she will let you borrow one from your school. If you need to order one, they are available from the biological supply companies listed in the For Further Information section at the back of this book.

Gather the water samples as described in Investigation 13 on page 86. Be sure there are no air bubbles in your samples. Stopper the samples immediately, preferably with the jar

Table 6   Dissolved Oxygen Levels

Site	Date	Time	Depth	Oxygen (mg/L)
Clear Lake	August 21	1:00 P.M.	50 centimeters (20 inches) below the surface	10 mg/L

or bottle still underwater. Do the tests as soon as possible because any change in temperature might affect your results. Record the data in your journal (see Table 6).

✔ Doing More

If you enjoy doing water testing, the book *Field Manual for Water Quality Monitoring: An Environmental Education Program for Schools* by Mark Mitchell and William Stapp (Thomson-Shore Inc., Dexter, MI) will give you detailed instructions on all the necessary procedures. Testing for such plant nutrients as nitrates and phosphorus can provide valuable information about the basic ecology of the pond, lake, or temporary pool you are investigating.

Underneath It All

As water flows into a lake or pond, it may have enough force to carry some of the material it encounters along with it. The material might range in size from large stones to gravel, sand, silt, or clay. When the water enters the lake or pond, the material it carries settles to the bottom. Larger materials settle faster than smaller things, so you can expect to find large rocks and stones close to

The fast-moving water in this stream carries large quantities of eroded material.

the shore. A lake may have a range of substrate types but ponds are usually limited to one kind of substrate.

Determining Substrate Types

You can add more features to the map you started in Project 10. Knowing what the substrate type is can help you find patterns in a lake. Do the plants grow where there are rocks or gravel? Or are you more likely to find them in areas with a substrate of mud or silt? How about insects? Some of them have claws for holding onto stones or gravel, so you can make a pretty good guess at where you'd find those. Fish prefer specific habitats too. Some species need rocks or stones to build their nests.

Using a shovel or hand trowel, scoop up some of the substrate from various sections of a lake or pond. Place the samples in plastic bags, marked with the location from which you took them. Refer to Table 7 to help you classify some of the substrate types that might give you trouble.

Table 7   Sand, Silt, or Clay

Soil Type	When the Soil Is Dry	When the Soil Is Wet
Sand	Falls apart when pressure is released	Can be formed but crumbles easily
Silt	Can be shaped and doesn't crumble easily	Forms a good cast; cannot be rolled into ribbon
Clay	Breaks into hard clots or lumps	Forms a thin ribbon

Making Comparisons, Finding Connections: A Look at Different Lakes and Ponds

One way to get a good feel for what makes your lake or pond unique is to compare it with others in your area. Try doing many of the same investigations and projects on another body of water—one that seems quite different from the one you are studying. For example, if you have been studying a fairly large lake, check out a farm pond. How do the two compare?

Record your data in your journal (see Table 8), including as much information as you can. What do the bodies of water have in common? What sets them apart?

Table 8 Lake or Pond Profile

Date	Lake or Pond	Water Temperature	Secchi Depth	Substrate Type	pH	Dissolved Oxygen	Fish	Plants	Remarks
August 30	Clear Lake	59°F (15°C)	13 feet (4 m)	Gravel	6.5	15 mg/L	Trout, bass	Cattails, saggitaria	After fall overturn
May 25	Miller's Pond	71°F (22°C)	2 feet (0.6 m)	Mud	8.5	5 mg/L	Sunfish	Cattails	Near farm

CHAPTER 5

Now and Then: Temporary Pools

DEPENDING ON THE TIME OF YEAR, temporary pools can be found in most parts of the United States. Though all the pools share a common trait—they fill with water at only certain times of the year— they have different names and characteristics depending on their location. In some places, people refer to these pools as **wetlands.** In the northern United States, these temporary bodies of water are sometimes called vernal pools. They are created primarily by spring snowmelt. In the southeastern United States, **Carolina bays** form after heavy spring rains. In the South and West, temporary pools may form after heavy rains. In the southwestern United States, these types of temporary pools are called playa lakes.

Underneath all these temporary pools lies a depression that will hold water. The depression fills with rain or snowmelt and because there are no streams or brooks

Some vernal pools may contain wood frogs and mole salamanders.

leading in or out, the water soon begins evaporating into the air or seeping into the ground. As a result, the pool begins to shrink in size. Usually these pools dry out completely within a few months.

This cycle of filling and drying presents great opportunities and challenges to a range of animals. With no waterways for fishes to enter, many of the animals here are protected from predators, but there are other challenges. They must complete their life cycle before the water is gone. As the pool shrinks, the creatures that live there are crowded into less space, and there is less oxygen to go around. The crowded creatures make an easy meal for predatory insects and visiting birds such as herons.

Temporary pools serve many important functions, but many people don't see their value. As a result, these pools are frequently drained and filled in to make room for farms and houses. When that happens, the pool creatures lose their home and local **biodiversity** is reduced. Increasingly, scientific research has helped us to realize the value of these pools. They help capture storm runoff and reduce flooding, and they even act as water purifiers—as water seeps into the groundwater from the pools, many of the contaminants it might contain are filtered out.

In many states, efforts are currently underway to locate, evaluate, and map these pools. Many schools have projects underway to identify and conserve the remaining pools.

Getting Acquainted with Life in Temporary Pools

Locate a vernal pool in the woods or fields around your home town. Try to estimate its size. Be sure to record the date and note the change in the size of the pool each time you visit. Use nets to sample the area for living things. You can use an aquarium net for the small invertebrates and a larger aquatic net for bigger animals such as frogs and salamanders.

Scoop up some mud and leaves from the bottom of the pool and examine it for any creatures that might be hiding there. You will probably have to examine the leaves closely with a hand lens to spot the smaller animals. Use a plastic spoon to scoop up individual crea-tures and put them in a white plastic pan or a cup so that you can get a better look at them. Use field guides and keys to help you identify what you find (see the For Further Information section for suggested keys).

A number of creatures can survive only in temporary pools. These creatures are called **ob-ligate species.** If these species are present, scientists classify a pool as a true vernal pool—in other words, it is large enough and lasts long enough for these obligate species to survive year after year. Wood frogs, which lay their eggs in temporary pools, are an obligate species. If the pools they live in are filled in, they vanish.

Explore temporary pools in your area for evidence of the fol-lowing obligate species: wood frogs, spotted salamanders, marbled salamanders, blue-spot-ted salamanders, Jefferson's salamanders, fairy shrimp, and spadefoot toads. Evidence may in-clude seeing the animals in the water, hearing the calls of the

Marbled salamanders breed in temporary pools that form in the autumn.

frogs coming from the pond, or finding the **spermato-phores**—or sperm packets—of the salamanders on leaves at the pond bottom.

You may find green frogs, leopard frogs, spring peepers, mayfly larvae, caddis fly larvae, mosquitoes, or dragonfly larvae in the pool as well. These species can live in a variety of ponds and lakes, as well as in temporary pools. They are called **facultative species.**

Don't worry if you can't identify all the creatures you find. With practice you'll soon learn to recognize more of them. Make a rough count of the number of species (and individuals of each species) that you find each time you visit. You may even want to plot these numbers and dates on a graph. Early in the life of a pool, you will find only a few species and few individuals of those species. As the season progresses, the number of species will increase but some of the early season species will become less abundant (or even disappear entirely). As that happens, however, new species will appear and increase in number. By tracking which animals increase and which animals decrease shortly afterward, you'll figure out which animals are predators and which are prey.

Examine some pond water under a compound microscope. (Perhaps you can borrow a microscope from your school science lab.) Do you find algae and other simple microorganisms that form the basis of the vernal pool food webs? Do the numbers of these tiny organisms change over time? Using your observations, try to create food webs for the species you find (see Figure 6 on page 28).

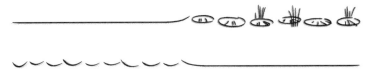

How Long Until I'm Grown, Mom?

When a temporary pool dries up most—if not all—of the adult animals within it die. But their offspring will return next year. Some of the larger creatures, like frogs and salamanders,

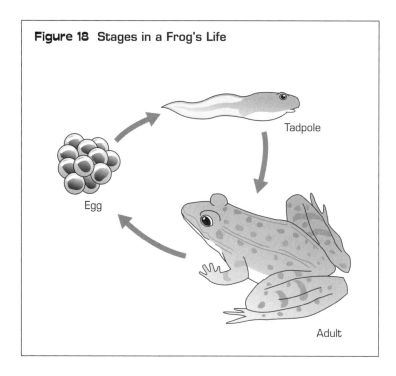

Figure 18 Stages in a Frog's Life

Tadpole

Egg

Adult

change from aquatic larvae to air-breathing, land-dwelling adult forms (see Figure 18). The change from gilled fishlike larvae or tadpoles to air-breathing adults happens at different rates depending on temperature, cloud cover, available oxygen, and other environmental conditions.

Different species also have different potential development times. In this project you'll compare the rates of development from egg to young adulthood by changing the conditions that might affect development. You'll also try to figure out if there are species whose development you can accelerate and others whose development remains constant. Changes in temperature, oxygen supply, food availability, predators, or parasites may all affect the development time of eggs and larvae, or determine whether they develop at all.

To figure out which—if any—of these **variables** affect development time, you'll need to set up an experiment to test each one. One of the easier variables to test is temperature.

To do this, you'll need at least six shallow pans to serve as aquariums and some frog or salamander eggs. Try finding these in a pool, or you can order them from a biological supply house (see the For Further Information section for ordering information). You'll also need six aquarium heaters, six aquarium air stones and pumps, six thermometers, and a waterproof marker.

To answer your questions about the relationship of temperature to development time, all the conditions in the aquariums, except the temperature, must be kept constant. For example, you'll need to be sure that oxygen, food supply, light, and any other variables you can think of stay the same. The only thing that should change is temperature. Set up the six aquariums in exactly the same way, or as close to it as possible. Use water from the vernal pool you are studying and fill each aquarium to within 1 inch (2.5 cm) of the top of the pan. (It might help to use the marker to draw a water line on each pan.) Place some stones and leaves on the bottom of the pan.

You will change the temperature in three aquariums by a few degrees. These pans are the **experimental group**—the group in which you are changing a variable to see what the effect will be. It is important to have several aquariums in each treatment group to be sure that what you might discover in one aquarium is not simply an accident. In three aquariums, no deliberate changes are made. These unchanged aquariums are the **control group** that will help you determine if changes you see in your animals are the result of the changes you made in their environment. Set up the aquarium heaters, pumps, air stones, and thermometers in all six pans.

Add eight eggs to each pan. You can work with a few more or less, but be sure to put the same number of eggs in each pan. Take the temperature of the vernal pool and record it. Heat the three treatment pans 3°C warmer than the pool. Try to keep the temperature of the control pans under conditions as much like the original pool as possible. You may even leave the pans at the pool site if they won't be disturbed, but you'll need access to electricity to heat the three experimental pans. Although it sounds easy to just raise the temperature by 3°C, you'll see that it is a challenging task. Temperature changes in response to light so you'll need to monitor your pans closely to keep the temperature constant. If you are finding it too difficult to control the temperature around the clock, try raising it for just a few hours each day. When scientists run large experiments in which they change the temperature, they might consider putting all of the treatment pans in a refrigerator set to a certain temperature, but then that changes the light the pans receive! You can see how a good scientist needs to think ahead to set up a properly controlled experiment.

If you have enough equipment, you can add another treatment group. Try making this group 6°C hotter than the control group. You can even try to test some variables other than temperature. For example, what happens if you don't use an air stone, or if you cut the water in the pan by half?

Monitor the development of your eggs and record the data in your journal (see Table 9). Note when legs first appear

Sample	Conditions/ Variables	Time to Hatching	Remarks
Table 9	**Egg Development and Temperature Change**		
Pan 1	Control		
Pan 2	Control		
Pan 3	Control		
Pan 4	+3°C water temperature		
Pan 5	+3°C water temperature		
Pan 6	+3°C water temperature		

on the larvae and when the gills disappear. Examine the various pans each day, preferably at the same time of day. Does the change in temperature affect the development time? The material on the bottom of the pans should create a supply of algae and protozoa in the pan upon which the hatchlings can feed. You may want to add some chopped spinach leaves to each pan to increase the food supply over the next few weeks.

Helping Your Temporary Pool

Temporary pools play an important role in the life cycles of many animals. They are also important to water quality. These areas often act as groundwater filters. Rainwater collects here and gradually seeps into the ground. As that happens, the plants in the pool help to clean the water by trapping the sediment and breaking down the chemicals and other impurities in the water. This helps prevent the pollutants from moving into rivers and other sources of drinking water. Temporary pools also help to control flooding, by slowing down moving water and providing a spot for it to trickle back down into the groundwater table.

Check with your state environmental offices and find out what kind of protection, if any, is provided for the conservation of temporary pools. Are developers required to identify temporary pools in the environmental impact statements that they need before they can go ahead with a project? Which agencies have jurisdiction in protecting these pools?

In some states, only vernal pools that have been formally certified are eligible for state protection. To be fully certified, vernal pools need to meet certain criteria. The pool must be an isolated basin that does not have a stream flowing into it or out of it for at least part of the year, and the pool must fill to a minimum volume and depth each year. The specific criteria may vary from state to state depending upon the state's

The plants in vernal pools and the soil they grow in remove pollutants from the water.

certification program. Check with the agency in your state that is responsible for protecting vernal pools—usually it is the non-game division of the state wildlife agency—to get the list of criteria. A number of high school students and classes around the country find and certify vernal pools. You can organize your own effort to find and register vernal pools in your area. Talk to your biology teacher to see if he or she might sponsor such an effort.

If you find yourself near a pool you think is worth saving, try some of the actions listed in Table 10 on the next page. Maybe you'll be able to "rescue" a pool before it's too late.

Table 10   Ways to Help a Temporary Pool

Action	Description
Write letters	Who needs to know that a vernal pool might be in danger of being lost? Write to the editor of your town's newspaper, local government officials, environmental clubs, or your local zoning board.
Start a petition	Gather the signatures of people interested in saving your temporary pool.
Organize a clean-up day	Ask your friends and family to help you clean up and take care of your temporary pool.
Attend meetings about the temporary pool	Are there plans to develop it? Has the public been allowed to comment on the plan or voice their opposition? Maybe no one at the meeting is aware of the value of your temporary pool; perhaps you can help educate them!
Start a newsletter	Maybe others can help you in your fight to save your temporary pool. Start a newsletter to keep people informed of your progress and to let them know how they can help.
Share your pool with other people	The more people who come to know and love the pool, the harder it might be to destroy it.

Tools and Equipment

You can put together a simple tool kit for exploring lakes, ponds, and temporary pools without spending a lot of money. You will probably find the following items useful in your investigations:

- white plastic or enamel pans for sorting what you find
- a ruler
- a magnifying glass or hand lens
- some collecting vials (medicine bottles, baby-food jars, or empty peanut butter jars work well)
- a small aquarium net
- thermometers for measuring air and water temperature
- preserving fluid, such as rubbing alcohol
- a medicine dropper or pipette
- access to a microscope

These basic supplies should get you started. For more in-depth investigations, you'll need to make some more specialized equipment using the following instructions.

Bottom Viewer

Looking for creatures at the bottom of a pond or lake can be tricky. This portable bottom viewer will make it a bit easier. To build a bottom viewer, you'll need a

Figure 19 Constructing a Bottom Viewer

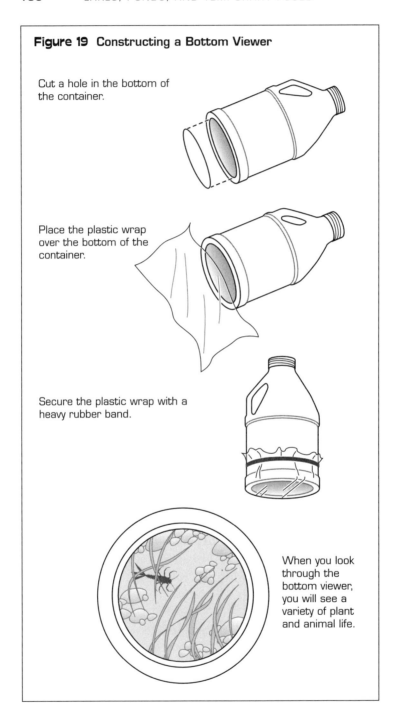

Cut a hole in the bottom of the container.

Place the plastic wrap over the bottom of the container.

Secure the plastic wrap with a heavy rubber band.

When you look through the bottom viewer, you will see a variety of plant and animal life.

clean, empty white bleach bottle, heavy plastic bucket, or 1-gallon milk container; heavy plastic wrap; a strong rubber band; a knife; and scissors.

Cut a hole about 1 inch from the edge of the container's bottom, as shown in Figure 19. (Ask an adult for help if you need to.) Cut a piece of plastic wrap 4 inches longer and wider than the bottom of the container, and secure it with the rubber band. If you are using a bleach bottle or milk bottle, wash it thoroughly and remove the cap from the container. Lower the plastic-covered end of the container into the water to see what swims by.

Plankton Net

To catch the tiniest stream animals, construct a net of silk or nylon (see Figure 20 on the next page). You'll need a plastic embroidery hoop that is 6 inches in diameter, scissors, a fishing swivel, three 1.5-ounce fishing weights, 10 feet of $\frac{1}{8}$-inch braided synthetic rope, and 4 feet of 30-pound test, monofilament fishing line.

The fabric you choose will determine how successful you are in netting plankton. Look for a lightweight, white or beige nylon or silk fabric with tightly woven threads. You want a fabric with mesh openings of 34 threads per inch. Use a hand lens or borrow a dissecting microscope from your school science lab to determine the size of the mesh opening of the fabric you choose. You'll need about $\frac{3}{4}$ yard of fabric to make the net.

Once you have chosen your fabric, cut a piece measuring 21 × 20 inches. Sew a small hem along one 21-inch edge. Then sew the two 20-inch edges together to form a cylinder. Attach the unhemmed edge of the cylinder to the inner ring of the embroidery hoop by bringing the fabric up through the center of the hoop and folding 1 inch of material over the edge of the inner hoop. Tuck the cut edge of the fabric back under itself, and use a needle and thread to sew the folded edge to the fabric just below the hoop. Snap the outer hoop around

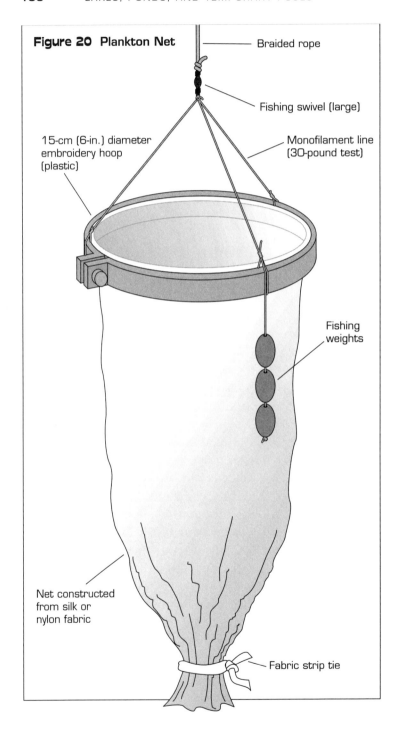

Figure 20 Plankton Net

Braided rope

Fishing swivel (large)

15-cm (6-in.) diameter embroidery hoop (plastic)

Monofilament line (30-pound test)

Fishing weights

Net constructed from silk or nylon fabric

Fabric strip tie

the inner embroidery hoop. Adjust the tightening screw to hold the net in place. Tie the other end of the cylinder closed with a strip of fabric or string.

To make a harness to tow the plankton net, cut three 20-inch pieces of fishing line. Attach one end of each piece to the outer ring of the embroidery hoop and space the pieces evenly around the ring. Tie the free end of each piece to a fishing swivel. Tie the braided rope to the other end of the swivel. When you tie the fishing line, be sure to make at least four knots to prevent it from coming undone.

Complete your net by adding three fishing weights to the outer hoop of the embroidery net with some fishing line. The weights help ensure that your net will sink so that you can get your sample.

Aquatic Net

To make an aquatic net to catch larger lake animals, you'll need the following materials: 4 feet of 3/4- or 1-inch wooden doweling, a strip of heavy canvas measuring 7×38 inches, 4 feet of 9-gauge galvanized wire, a mesh laundry bag that is 17 inches long with a 21-inch diameter opening and a mesh size of $\frac{1}{4}$-inch or less, two stainless steel hose clamps $\frac{9}{16}$- to $1\frac{1}{4}$-inch, a sewing machine or needle and thread, an iron and ironing board, a measuring tape, a marker, a utility knife, pliers, a hammer, a screwdriver, a drill, and a $\frac{7}{32}$-inch drill bit. Hose clamps can be purchased at a hardware or autoparts store. An old mop handle can be used in place of the wooden dowel.

To make the frame, determine the exact center of the length of wire (see Figure 21 on the next page). Bend the wire at the indicated points. Work on a flat surface, and use pliers to make the bends. Clip the free ends of the wire $\frac{1}{2}$ inch from the last bend. With your hands, round the two 13.5-inch sections while bringing the two cut ends together, forming a shape like the letter D.

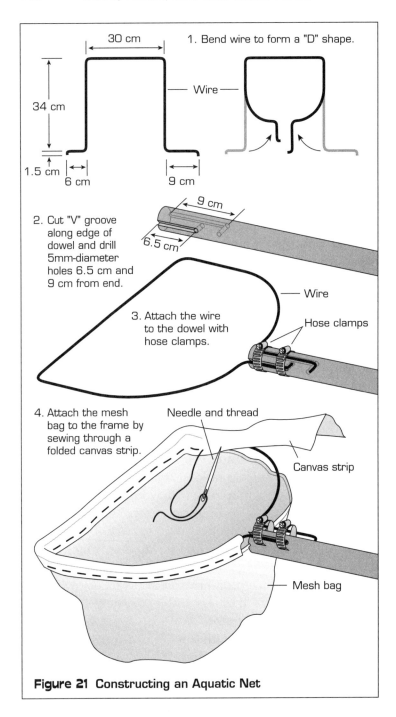

30 cm

1. Bend wire to form a "D" shape.

Wire

34 cm

1.5 cm
6 cm

9 cm

2. Cut "V" groove along edge of dowel and drill 5mm-diameter holes 6.5 cm and 9 cm from end.

9 cm

6.5 cm

Wire

3. Attach the wire to the dowel with hose clamps.

Hose clamps

4. Attach the mesh bag to the frame by sewing through a folded canvas strip.

Needle and thread

Canvas strip

Mesh bag

Figure 21 Constructing an Aquatic Net

To attach the mesh laundry bag to the metal frame, fold under the edges of the canvas strip $\frac{1}{2}$ inch and press with an iron. Now fold the fabric in half lengthwise, and press again. Drape the strip over the frame along the pressed fold. Sandwich the edge of the laundry bag opening between the two pieces of canvas. Using the needle and thread, sew the canvas strip to the mesh bag.

Prepare the handle by drilling a hole $\frac{7}{32}$ inch in diameter $3\frac{1}{2}$ inches from one end of the dowel. Rotate the dowel 180 degrees and drill a second hole $2\frac{1}{2}$ inches from the end of the dowel. With a utility knife, cut two shallow, V-shaped grooves from each hole to the end of the rod. The grooves should be just deep enough to snugly fit the wire you used for the framing. Fit the shaped net frame to the handle and drive the wire ends into the drilled openings with a hammer. To secure the net to the doweling, slide two hose clamps over the handle. Use a screwdriver to tighten the hose clamps.

Secchi Disk

Secchi disks can be purchased, but they are relatively easy to make. You'll need a 1-gallon paint-can lid, one $\frac{5}{16}$ - × 4- inch eye-bolt, two $\frac{5}{16}$-inch nuts, two $\frac{5}{16}$-inch washers, three 3- × $3\frac{1}{4}$-inch anchor-bolt washers, a waterproof marker, masking tape, a tape measure, a 66-foot length of $\frac{1}{4}$-inch synthetic fiber rope, black and white enamel paint, a hammer, and a screwdriver (see Figure 22 on the next page).

Wash the paint-can lid to remove any dried paint. Divide the top surface into four quadrants using a ruler and a marker. With masking tape, mask off two quadrants that are opposite each other. Paint the exposed quadrants with black paint and allow them to dry. Remove the masking tape and cover the black quadrants. Paint the remaining two quadrants white.

When the paint is dry, use a hammer and screwdriver to punch a small hole in the center of the lid. It should

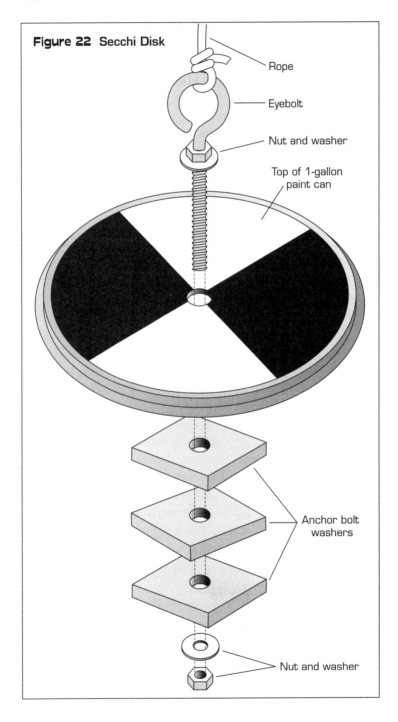

Figure 22 Secchi Disk

Rope

Eyebolt

Nut and washer

Top of 1-gallon paint can

Anchor bolt washers

Nut and washer

be just large enough to accommodate the eyebolt. Be sure to bend the sharp edges back and hammer them down after punching the hole. Thread a nut and then a washer onto the eyebolt. Push the eyebolt through the hole in the paint-can lid, and position it so that the eye of the eyebolt is exposed to the painted side of the lid. Add three anchor-bolt washers, one small washer, and a nut to the eyebolt. Tighten the nut so that the anchor-bolt washers fit tightly against the underside of the lid.

To make the calibrated line used to lower the disk into the water, tie a rope to the eye of the eyebolt so that the Secchi disk hangs horizontally. Using a tape measure or yardstick, measure 20 inches from the surface of the disk along the rope. Use a waterproof marker to mark this spot on the rope. Continue marking the rope every 20 inches to a final length of 66 feet.

Plant Hook

A plant hook can be used to retrieve submerged aquatic plants from areas of a lake that are too deep to wade in. To make a plant hook, you'll need two metal coat hangers, a piece of metal piping that is 1 inch wide and 5 inches long, one $\frac{1}{2}$-inch nut and washer, wire snips, and a short piece of rope (see Figure 23 on the next page).

Take apart the coat hangers and straighten the wires. Cut each wire in half for a total of four 20-inch pieces. Fold each piece in half, and then fold $\frac{1}{4}$ inch of each looped end back on itself. Insert the cut ends of wire through the center of the metal piping and hook the bent loops over the piping edge. Now bend the cut ends of the coat hanger toward the piping.

Thread a washer and a nut onto the rope. Tie several knots behind the nut. Thread the free end of the rope through the bottom of the plant hook, and pull it out the top. Pull the nut and washer tight against the wire pieces. Use the short rope to attach the device to a longer piece of rope.

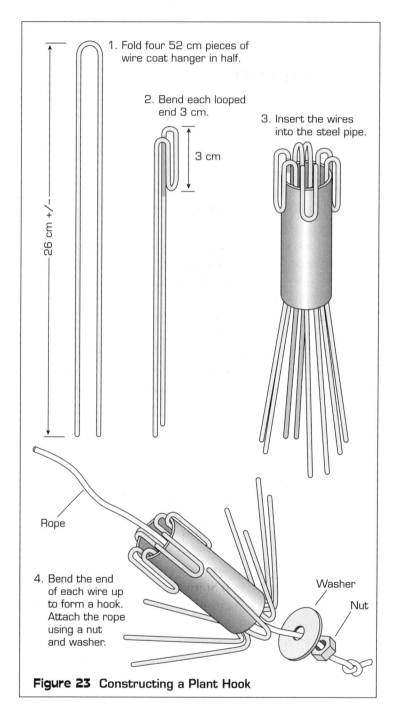

1. Fold four 52 cm pieces of wire coat hanger in half.

2. Bend each looped end 3 cm.

3 cm

3. Insert the wires into the steel pipe.

26 cm +/-

Rope

4. Bend the end of each wire up to form a hook. Attach the rope using a nut and washer.

Washer

Nut

Figure 23 Constructing a Plant Hook

Glossary

acidic—having a pH below 7.0

aerobic—living, active, or occurring in the presence of oxygen

algae—mostly one-celled, photosynthetic organisms belonging to the protist kingdom

alkaline—salts of various minerals dissolved in water or in soil deposits

amphibian—a group of animals that spend part of their life in water and part on land. The young have gills and are fishlike in appearance. As they grow, they develop legs and begin to breathe through lungs.

anaerobic—living, active, or occurring in the absence of oxygen

basic—having a pH above 7.0

benthic—of, pertaining to, or living on the bottom of a body of water

biodiversity—all the organisms living in an area

bloom—a sudden overgrowth, usually of algae

brackish—a mixture of freshwater and saltwater

caldera—a water-filled, hollowed-out bowl of a dormant volcano

Carolina bay—a freshwater seasonal pool found in the southeastern United States

cercus (plural **cerci**)—either of a pair of sensory tails on the last abdominal segment of many insects

contour interval—the distance between contour lines on a topographic map that indicates a change in elevation

contour line—lines on topographic maps that join points of equal elevation on the surface

control group—a test group used for the basis of comparison where no experimental factors are introduced

crustacean—any of a class of arthropods that lives in the water and breathes through gills. This group includes crawfish, lobsters, and shrimps

density—the mass of a substance per unit of volume

dichotomous—characterized by repeated branching or forking

divide—a high point surrounding a body of water, marking one of the boundaries of its watershed

ecologist—a scientist who studies the interrelationships between organisms and their environment

ecology—the study of the interrelationships among organisms and their environment

ecosystem—a natural community of organisms and their environment

emergent plant—a plant that grows well with its roots wet, but its leaves and flowers above water

entomologist—a person who studies insects

epilimnion—the less dense and warmer upper layer of a stratified lake

eutrophic—a lake with a large supply of nutrients and a diverse assemblage of life

evaporation—the process by which water re-enters Earth's atmosphere

experimental group—in a controlled experiment, the group on which a variable is being tested

facultative species—a species that thrives in a variety of environments

food web—a network of living organisms linked by their feeding relationships

glacial moraine deposit—debris at the edge of a glacier that once covered land

groundwater—freshwater below the Earth's surface

hypolimnion—the lower, cooler layer of a stratified lake

hypothermia—a condition that occurs when a person's body temperature drops below normal levels. Hypothermia is characterized by slowed body activity and mental malfunctioning. It can easily result in death.

inorganic—a chemical compound that comes from non-living matter

key—an aid to classification or identification

larva (plural **larvae**)—an active immature stage in an animal's life history

lentic—pertaining to still waters, such as lakes, ponds, or bogs

limnetic zone—an open-water area away from the shore

limnologist—a scientist who studies freshwater environments

littoral zone—a shallow-water area along the shore

mesotrophic—a term for lakes that have a moderate supply of nutrients

metalimnion—the transition layer between the epilimnion and the hypolimnion of a stratified lake

morphological—pertaining to the structure or form of an organism

naiad—a specific term for the nymphs of dragonflies and damselflies

niche—the role an organism plays in its environment

nutrient—dissolved minerals and organic materials that wash into a body of water from the surrounding land and provide nourishment for living things

obligate species—a creature that can survive only in temporary pools that have no fish

oligotrophic—a lake that has limited nutrients

organic—a chemical or other substance derived from living matter

oxbow lake—a lake formed when a river changes course, leaving an isolated body of water

perpendicular—at a 90-degree angle

photosynthesis—the process by which plants use sunlight, carbon dioxide, and water to form sugars and oxygen

plankton—microscopic plant and animal life that drifts in the water

playa lake—a temporary lake that forms after heavy rains, primarily in desert regions

profundal zone—the deepest zone in lakes and ponds, where no sunlight penetrates

radula—the mouthparts of snails that consist of a circular row of teeth to scrape algae and other material for food

respiration—the process by which tissues and organisms exchange gases with their environment

siphon—a tube used by mollusks such as clams and mussels for taking in water and food

spermatophore—a packet of sperm deposited by a male salamander

stipule—a winglike or scalelike organ attached to the base of the leaf petiole or on the stem where the leaf attaches

submergent plant—a plant in a pond or lake that is totally submerged except for its flowering parts

substrate—material at the bottom of a lake or pond, or any surface upon which organisms grow

surface tension—the attraction of water molecules to each other at the water's surface

taxonomy—the rules for and process of classifying organisms

tectonic—a geological force involving changes to Earth's crust

thermocline—the more common term for the metalimnion or transition layer in a stratified lake

topographic map—a map that shows land features, such as hills, valleys, streams, ponds, and marshes

transect line—in mapping, a line that runs from a baseline, along which distances to various features of the landscape are measured

variable—any one of the many different conditions that affect the activity of living or non-living parts of the environment

vernal pool—a temporary pool that forms primarily in spring from snowmelt and early spring rains

watershed—the land drained by a river or stream and all its tributaries

water-tolerant plant—a plant that can tolerate having its roots and stem in water but needs to have its leaves in the air

wetland—an area that is covered with water for at least part of the year

For Further Information

Books

Doris, Ellen. *Woods, Ponds, and Fields*. New York: Thames & Hudson, 1994.

Gardner, Robert. *Where on Earth Am I?* Danbury, CT: Franklin Watts, 1996.

Hjellström, B. *Be Expert with Map and Compass*. New York: Macmillan, 1994.

Kellogg, L.L. *Monitor's Guide to Aquatic Macroinvertebrates*. 2nd ed. Gaithersburg, MD: Izaak Walton League of America, 1994.

Lewis, B.A. *The Kid's Guide to Social Action: How to Solve the Social Problems You Choose—And Turn Creative Thinking Into Positive Action*. Minneapolis, MN: Free Spirit Publishing, Inc., 1991.

McCafferty, W.P. *Aquatic Entomology: The Fishermen's and Ecologists' Illustrated Guide to Insects and Their Relatives*. Boston: Science Books International, 1981.

Merritt, Richard W. and Kenneth W. Cummins. *Introduction to Aquatic Insects*, 2nd ed. Dubuque, IA: Kendall/Hunt Publishing Company, 1984.

Moyle, Peter B. *Fish: An Enthusiast's Guide*. Berkeley: University of California Press, 1993.

Page, Lawrence M. and Brooks M. Burr. *Peterson Field Guide to Freshwater Fishes*. Boston: Houghton Mifflin, 1991.

Rainis, Kenneth G. and Bruce J. Russell. *Guide to Microlife*. Danbury, CT: Franklin Watts, 1997.

Redington, Charles B. *Plants in Wetlands.* Dubuque, IA: Kendall Hunt Publishing Company, 1994.

Reid, G.K. *Pond Life. A Guide to Common Plants and Animals of North American Ponds and Lakes.* New York: Golden Press, 1987.

Agencies and Organizations

American Society of Limnology and Oceanography
3400 Bosque Boulevard, Suite 680
Waco, TX 76710-4446

American Water Works Association
Public Information Department
6666 West Quincy Ave.
Denver, CO 80235

United States Environmental Protection Agency (EPA)
Water Resources Center
401 M Street SW
Washington, DC 20460

Equipment Suppliers

Carolina Biological Supply Company
2700 York Rd.
Burlington, NC 27215-3398
Live water striders can be purchased from March through November.

LaMotte Company
P.O. Box 329
Chestertown, MD 21620
This company specializes in equipment and test kits for the analysis of water, soil, and air.

Wildlife Supply Company
301 Cass St.
Saginaw, MI 48602
A company that specializes in aquatic sampling instruments and equipment.

United States Geological Survey (USGS)
Information Services
P.O. Box 25286
Denver Federal Center
Denver, CO 80255
You can order a topographic map of the area you wish to explore from the USGS. Be as specific as possible about the location you want the map for—include state, county, town, and if you are interested in a particular lake, include its name.

Internet Resources

American Society of Limnology and Oceanography
http://www.aslo.org
The official website for the ASLO organization. The site has a lot of links to fish, aquatic plant, and invertebrate sites.

Center for Aquatic Plants
http://aquat1.ifas.ufl.edu/
This website, sponsored by University of Florida Center for Aquatic and Invasive Plants, features photographs and descriptions of most of the aquatic and wetlands plants found in the United States.

The Evergreen Project—Lakes and Ponds
http://mbgnet.mobot.org/fresh/lakes/index.htm
This site, sponsored by the Missouri Botanical Garden, features aerial photographs of many North American lakes and ponds, and some common lake inhabitants.

Guide to Limnology
http://library.advanced.org/11548/limn.html
A website offering basic limnology information, including descriptions of the most common water-quality tests.

North American Benthological Society
http://www.benthos.org
Official website for the NABS scientific organization, with links to other freshwater-oriented websites, including many college and university webpages.

North American Lake Management Society
http://www.nalms.org
The site features a glossary of common lake and pond terms, and information on how you can participate in the Great American Secchi dip-in!

Index

About the Author

David Josephs has been an elementary and high school science teacher, a textbook editor, and a science curriculum developer. He has also written more than twenty books on natural history and environmental education topics and published numerous magazine and journal articles.

Mr. Josephs is now semi-retired and spends his time working with digital cameras, carving wildlife in wood, hiking, and canoeing around the pond near his home in Massachusetts. One day, he would like to build a replica of Stonehenge in his backyard.